God's Hand in
Life's Little Moments

God's Hand in Life's Little Moments

Written by Julie Grosz, M.Ed.

Editor:
Carrie Austin

Cover Designer:
Merlin DeBoer

Scriptures taken from the HOLY BIBLE, NEW INTERNATIONAL VERSION. NIV. Copyright 1973, 1978, 1984 International Bible Society. Used by permission of Zondervan. All rights reserved.

Copyright 2005 by Julie Grosz
Little Moments Publishing

Website: www.heartofdakota.com

All rights reserved. No part of this book may be stored in a retrieval system, reproduced or transmitted in any form or by any means – graphic, electronic, mechanical, photocopying, recording, or otherwise – without prior written permission from the author.

Printed in the U.S.A.

ISBN 0-9747695-6-8

DEAR READER,

Come in, friend. Have a seat, and put your feet up for a while. Can I get you something to drink? Maybe some spiced tea, hot chocolate, or flavored coffee? Those are my favorites, but you can have whatever fits your fancy. I know you won't be able to stay long, but there's Someone that's been waiting for you, and He's missed you lately or you wouldn't be holding this book. He has many different names, but He's your Friend, your Father, and your Savior all wrapped up in One, and nothing makes Him happier than spending time with you. Go ahead and sip your drink as you peruse the *Prepare Your Heart* page of this devotional. Did you notice a theme, connecting the different roles of your life together? Just like your Visitor, you have many different names too, like *Christian woman, wife, mother*, and *teacher* of your children. It's a big responsibility being all those things, but there's some people who have gone before you that can help. Your Visitor wants you to get to know them, that's why He wrote His amazing book called the Bible. These people are a lot like you, and much can be learned from reading about their lives. Each day you'll meet someone new, and each person has been hand-picked to fit your roles in life. You'll meet Christian women, married couples, mothers, and people from Jesus' Parables. These people are interesting, and they are worth getting to know. One last person you'll get to know is me, and I think you'll find I'm a lot like you. I've shared my life with you in this book, and you'll see I need to read this book just as much as you do. Please enjoy the *quote, my personal stories, a Bible connection, a few questions, some music*, and the *prayers*. It's time for me to go now. I have my own personal time with your Visitor too, and I don't like to keep Him waiting. So settle in for a little while, before someone needs you desperately – as they always do – and spend some little moments with your Visitor, our Lord and Savior. He's waiting for you…

Table of Contents

Dedication

Acknowledgments

Introduction

> **KEY:** **Role #1** = Christian Woman
> **Role #2** = Wife
> **Role #3** = Mother
> **Role #4** = Teacher of Your Children

Chapter One: Attitude
    Role #1: An Attitude of Reverence
    Role #2: A "Willing to Help" Attitude
    Role #3: A Persistent Attitude
    Role #4: Attitude Is a Choice

Chapter Two: Meaningful Relationships
    Role #1: Knowing What's Needed Most
    Role #2: Filling Each Other's Needs
    Role #3: Grandma's Legacy of Faith
    Role #4: A Strong Sense of Security

Chapter Three: Attraction
    Role #1: Getting Caught Up in Appearances
    Role #2: Attraction That Endures
    Role #3: Attraction to Trouble
    Role #4: Appearing to Be Perfect

Chapter Four: Stress and Pressure
    Role #1: The Pressure of Using Time Wisely
    Role #2: Trying to Be an Excellent Wife
    Role #3: When to Say "Yes" and When to Say "No"
    Role #4: What Are You Busy Doing?

Chapter Five: Strength of Character
    Role #1: Being a Light in Any Situation
    Role #2: Taking a Different Approach
    Role #3: A Strong Faith to Walk the Walk
    Role #4: A Firm Foundation

Chapter Six: Shortcomings
　Role #1: Mistakes, Shortcomings, and Sins
　Role #2: Overreacting Gets Us Nowhere
　Role #3: Wanting God's Best for Our Children
　Role #4: Even Superwoman Had Shortcomings
Chapter Seven: Differences
　Role #1: We're Not So Different After All
　Role #2: Different Ways of Thinking
　Role #3: Differences in Children
　Role #4: Being Different vs. Fitting In
Chapter Eight: Jealousy, Envy, and Greed
　Role #1: Jealousy, Envy, and Greed
　Role #2: Jealous of His Interests
　Role #3: Jealous of "Dad Being the Favorite"
　Role #4: The Cost of Jealousy and Greed
Chapter Nine: Worry
　Role #1: Worrying Accomplishes Nothing
　Role #2: Worrying about Relatives
　Role #3: Worrying – Will They Turn Out Right?
　Role #4: Worrying about Our Children's Faith
Chapter Ten: Sadness
　Role #1: Sadness and Regrets about Past Sins
　Role #2: Not a Fairy Tale Marriage
　Role #3: The Comfort of a Mother's Arms
　Role #4: Caring for One Another
Chapter Eleven: Confusion
　Role #1: Confused about How to Solve a Problem
　Role #2: Confusion Caused by Poor Communication
　Role #3: When Your Children Are Confused
　Role #4: Confused about What's Right and Wrong
Chapter Twelve: Thoughts
　Role #1: Thoughtful Thoughts
　Role #2: Thoughts Often Become Words
　Role #3: Thoughts about Being a Mother
　Role #4: Self-Absorbed Thoughts

Chapter Thirteen: Achievement
    Role #1: God Deserves Credit for Achievements
    Role #2: Achieving a Common Direction in Marriage
    Role #3: How to Achieve Success
    Role #4: The Achievement of "Being Somebody"

Chapter Fourteen: Organization
    Role #1: Little Changes Make Big Differences
    Role #2: Be Deliberate in Your Actions
    Role #3: Planning to Protect Our Children
    Role #4: It's Not Enough Just to Want Something

Chapter Fifteen: Anger
    Role #1: Why Is This Happening?
    Role #2: Being Calm When a Mistake Has Been Made
    Role #3: When Children Are Wayward
    Role #4: Habits Are Hard to Break

Chapter Sixteen: Love
    Role #1: Loving Our Father, with All of Our Heart
    Role #2: Proof of Love
    Role #3: A Mother's Love
    Role #4: Lasting Love

Chapter Seventeen: Trust
    Role #1: Trust in the Lord
    Role #2: Trusting Your Marriage Partner
    Role #3: Trusting the Engineer
    Role #4: Who Can Be Trusted to Teach Our Children?

Chapter Eighteen: Time for Joy
    Role #1: Unexpected Joy and Humor
    Role #2: Finding Joy in Marriage
    Role #3: The Right and Wrong Time to Laugh
    Role #4: Finding Joy in Teaching about God

Final Letter

Scripture References

My Family Legacy (in pictures)

Resources

This book is dedicated to my loving family...

Kenneth Corwin Mellema...my father
Marlene Fay Mellema...my mother
Richard Edward Grosz...my husband
Wyatt James Grosz...my son
Riley Kenneth Grosz...my son
David William Madden...my brother-in-law
Cindy Lee Madden...my sister
Michael Robert Austin...my brother-in-law
Carrie Lynn Austin...my sister

Elizabeth, Joshua, Abigail,
Aaron, Rachel, & Anna Madden
Cole, Shaw, & Greyson Austin
...my neices and nephews

~ The Lord has richly blessed my life
through the gift of family.

Acknowledgments

My Lord and Savior, Jesus Christ...
For teaching me Your ways, one little moment at a time,
and for patiently loving me through it all.
It is my prayer that You may be glorified through this work.

My Parents, Ken and Marlene Mellema...
For passing on the legacy of your faith, and for making family
a priority. For the laughs, the tears, the talks,
the hugs, and most of all, the memories made together.

My Sister, Carrie...
For being my support in times of need,
my confidant in times of stress, and my friend
to laugh with in times of joy. For editing this book,
and lending a logical ear to this emotional girl.

My Sister, Cindy...
For being my fellow emotional girl,
for listening patiently, and for giving me sound advice.
For having a God-honoring vision for your family,
and for passing that vision on to the rest of us.

My Brother-in-Law, Mike...
For being more like a brother than a brother-in-law,
and for all the behind-the-scenes work you do
for the business side of writing and publishing a book.

My Husband, Rich...
For loving and caring for me in your own special way.
For providing for our family. For loving our children as only a
father can, and for filling our home with laughter.

My Sons, Wyatt and Riley...
For lighting up my life with sweet smiles, giggly laughs,
messy kisses, silly questions, and profound moments
of seeing God's world through your eyes.
For teaching me to love in an entirely different way.

Introduction

You may be wondering if this is the right devotional for you. That's a good question, so let's find out the answer! Please answer "yes" or "no" to each of these questions:
1. Are you a Christian woman?
2. Are you a wife?
3. Are you a mother?
4. Are you trying to teach your children about God?

If your answer was "yes" to each of these questions, this devotional and you are a match made in heaven!

You may also be wondering what a week in this devotional looks like. That's another good question! So, here's a …

Sneak Peek at a Week…

Each week has a different theme, and the theme begins with a quote to set the mood. Next, the "Prepare Your Heart" page gives a simple overview of the 5-day theme.

Days 1, 2, 3, and 4 all have these features…

Quote: Begin each day with a special quote that is expressly chosen to fit each of your roles in life.
Personal Story: Read stories that warm your heart, tickle your funny bone, and draw you closer to God.
Bible Connection: Meet some fascinating people from the Bible, and learn how their stories are similar to yours.
(Note: These Bible stories are written as part of the devotional, but Scriptures are also listed if you'd like to look them up.)
Personal Connection: Make some meaningful connections between the Bible and your life.
A Welcome Retreat: Share a simple prayer, ponder one thought-provoking question, and listen to a special song.
(Note: Choose contemporary or traditional music. The "Prepare Your Heart" page shows how the music connects to the theme.)

DAYS 1, 2, 3, AND 4 focus on different roles of life:
Day 1 – Christian Woman: Links your life with the lives of women from the Bible. The prayer is personal.
Day 2 – Wife: Links your life with the lives of couples from the Bible. The prayer is shared with your husband. *(Note: These are very simple prayers. If you've never prayed with your husband, this is an easy way to start.)*
Day 3 – Mother: Links your life with the lives of mothers from the Bible. The prayer is shared with your children. *(Note: This is an excellent way to show your children you pray for them consistently.)*
Day 4 – Teacher of Your Children: Links your teaching with Jesus' parables. The prayer is shared with your children. *(Note: This is a terrific way to show your children the Christian character qualities you want them to have in their life.)*

DAY 5 gives you time to reflect on the theme...
There is one question for you to consider for each of your roles in life. Then, you say a simple prayer and listen to the music selection one more time as a closure to the theme.

A Few Final Thoughts...

This devotional addresses common things you deal with in everyday life. I wrote this devotional so you can finish the book part in about 10 minutes because women who have all of these roles in life are especially busy. However, it is my prayer that you will think of the theme often throughout your day and week, as the little moments of your life bring connections to mind. I pray that these connections draw you closer to God, and I pray that the Lord is glorified through your time spent with Him.

Love in Christ,
Julie Grosz

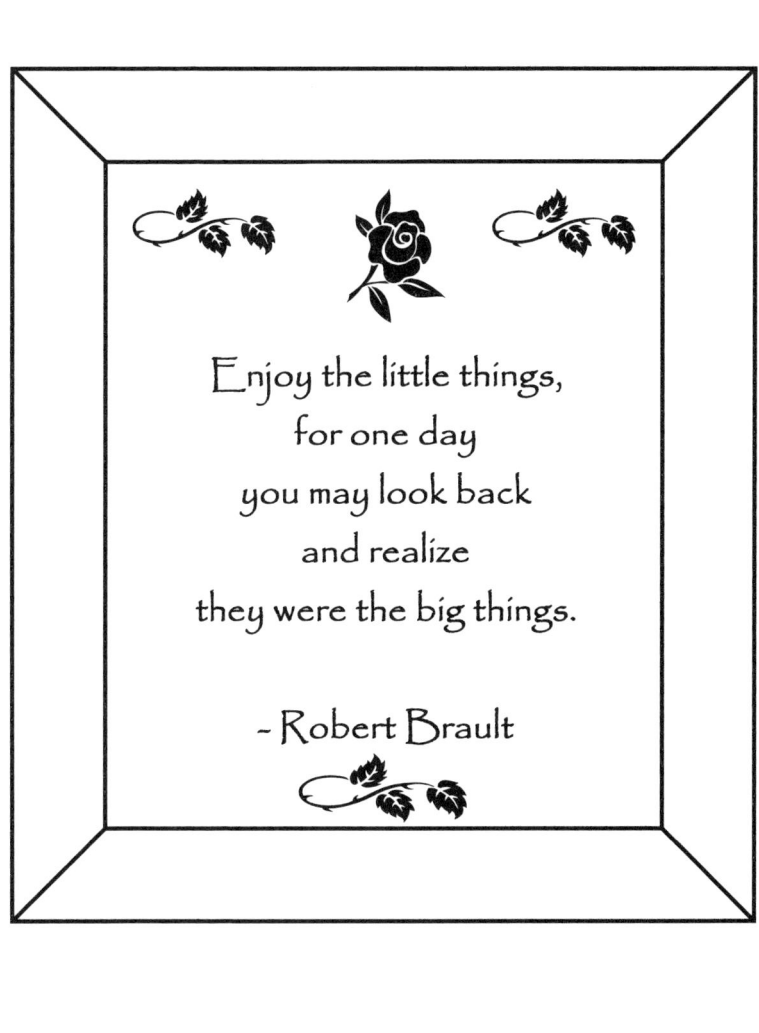

Prepare Your Heart

Prayer:
As a Christian woman, a wife, a mother, and a teacher, please help my attitude to be pleasing to You.

Role #1: Christian Woman
An Attitude of Reverence

Role #2: Wife
A "Willing to Help" Attitude

Role #3: Mother
A Persistent Attitude

Role #4: Teacher
Attitude Is a Choice

Contemporary Music Connection:
"Let It Rain"
Even the earth trembles at the Lord's command because He reigns over all. The Lord's Creation reveals His glory, and your attitude toward Him for even the gift of your life should be reverent and joyful.

Traditional Music Connection:
"I Need You"
You need God in your life. Your attitude should reflect total dependence on Him.

Chapter 1: Day 1

An Attitude of Reverence

> Wonder is the attitude of reverence for the infinite values and meaning of life, and of marveling over God's purpose and patience in it all.
> - George W. Fiske

One Sunday each month, our church has a special tradition. A large plastic jug is set out on the stage in the front of the church. As young children flock to the stage for the children's sermon, they bring pennies to place in the jug. Over time, hundreds of dollars have been collected from the pennies children have placed in the jug. Many church programs have benefited from the seemingly small offerings of pennies that children have given over the years.

I love to hear the clinking of pennies as they are dropped in the jug, and the angelic looks on the children's faces remind me of how we should also feel it is a privilege and an honor to give to the Lord. A feeling of wonder and reverence for the Lord washes over me as I remember how God's already worked in many of these children's lives.

I remember how God healed a child with clubfeet so perfectly that you'd never know he once struggled to walk. I recollect how God stretched His hand halfway across the world to bring two beautiful children here to be adopted by a loving couple. I recall how God stopped children from being born prematurely time and time again to create strong and healthy children, rather than weak and underdeveloped ones. As I see a child who once struggled to take each breath bounding up the steps of the stage to drop her pennies in the jar, I'm reminded we don't have to look far to see how much respect God deserves. If we all had the attitude children have as they give their pennies, we'd be closer to showing God a portion of the reverence He is due.

BIBLE CONNECTION:
A POOR WIDOW HAS A REVERENT ATTITUDE

A poor widow came to the place where offerings were given and put in two very small copper coins, worth only a fraction of a penny. Calling his disciples to him, Jesus said, "I tell you the truth, this poor widow has put more into the treasury than all the others. They all gave out of their wealth; but she, out of her poverty, put in all she had to live on." (Mark 12:42-44)

PERSONAL CONNECTION
ROLE #1: CHRISTIAN WOMAN

This woman was poverty-stricken. By giving away the last of her coins, she showed a complete attitude of reverence toward the Lord. Even though her gift was meager, Jesus found it noteworthy enough to tell His disciples about it. As Christian women, let's be like this woman and have an unwavering attitude of reverence toward God. Even when things go wrong, we can choose an attitude that is right.

   A WELCOME RETREAT

Prayer to Share: *Lord, I'm in awe of You! Please help me to have an unwavering reverent attitude toward You.*
Question: Do you remember to have an attitude of reverence toward the Lord, even when life is hard?
Contemporary Music – *Worship* CD:
  Song Title: *"Let It Rain"* – Track 8
Traditional Music – *Ryman Gospel Reunion* CD:
  Song Title: *"I Need You"* – Track 15

Chapter 1: Day 2

A "Willing to Help" Attitude

> I know some good marriages – marriages where both people are just trying to get through their days by helping each other, being good to each other.
> - Erica Jong

I was in my flannel pajamas and fuzzy slippers when something swooped down and grazed the top of my head. I screamed a blood-curdling shriek, and Rich stumbled out of the bathtub to see what was wrong. He was dripping water everywhere. We both hit the floor as the creature made another swoop. It landed in a corner, and we both shuddered as we realized we had a bat in the house.

I grabbed the nearest weapon, which happened to be a fish net. On the next swoop, I wildly waved the net at the bat as Rich yelled, "Net him, Julie!" My aim was pretty shaky, since I was lying facedown and not looking at the target. After several failed attempts, Rich and I made a new plan to turn on all of the lights except in the bathroom.

The minute the lights came on, the bat shot into the dark bathroom, and Rich slammed the door. Rich's hunting instincts *finally* kicked in. He grabbed a BB gun and dashed outside of the house to the bathroom window. His aim was pretty unsteady, and he had a window screen to shoot through, but my man came through and shot the bat in two shots.

Our bathroom ceiling still has two little holes in it. They remind us of that time we were willing to help each other with a problem that neither one of us wanted to solve alone.

Bible Connection: Acsah and Her Husband Work Together

Caleb gave his daughter Acsah in marriage to his younger brother as a reward for capturing his enemies. Although Acsah didn't choose her mate, she chose a helpful attitude by working with him to acquire good land and water. Acsah urged her husband to ask Caleb for a field. Her husband did, and Caleb gave them a field, but it was very dry. So when Caleb asked what he could do for Acsah she said, "Please give us water to go with our land." Then, Caleb gave them the upper and lower springs. (Judges 1:12-15)

Personal Connection
Role #2: Wife

Acsah's "willing to help" attitude enabled her and her husband to acquire good land and water. As wives, choosing a helpful attitude toward our husbands goes a long way. Sometimes, all we really need to do to be able to reclaim a fresh attitude is to know we're not "in it alone". Let's get through our days by helping each other, and by being good to each other. In doing so, we'll have a set of memories with our husbands that are special enough to turn our *union* into a *marriage*.

 A Welcome Retreat

Prayer to Share (with husband): *Help me work together with my husband, so we can depend on each other when we need help.*
Question: Would you say you and your husband have a helpful attitude toward one another?
Contemporary Music – *Worship* CD:
 Song Title: *"Let It Rain"* – Track 8
Traditional Music – *Ryman Gospel Reunion* CD:
 Song Title: *"I Need You"* – Track 15

 CHAPTER 1: DAY 3

A PERSISTENT ATTITUDE

> Whatever course you decide upon, there is always someone to tell you that you are wrong. There are always difficulties arising which tempt you to believe your critics are right. To map out a course of action and follow it to an end requires…courage.
> - Ralph Waldo Emerson

It was only 9:30 AM, and I already had a migraine headache. Riley, our 8 month old, was crying nonstop. Wyatt, our 4 ½ year old, was talking nonstop. I packed the suburban to get out of the house, but when I turned the key, nothing happened. The battery was dead, and I dejectedly realized I was stranded. I began thinking *Why did I decide to stay home instead of having a career?*

At lunch, Riley threw his food on the floor and smeared the rest of it in his hair. Wyatt loudly sang songs that made no sense, and Ruby, our puppy, began barking very loudly. When I told her, *No, no!* she turned my full-length skirt into a mini-skirt with one big rip. I was standing in the kitchen half-dressed, trying to fix my skirt, when Rich called to say he'd be late, and that's when I smelled the cookies burning.

I won't torture you with any more "bad day, bad attitude" lamenting, especially since that day just kept getting worse. On bad days, I try to refocus on why God first led me to stay home instead of having a career. When God laid it on my heart to stay home, I knew there'd be bad days. I knew I'd need God's help to follow it through. With this kind of thinking, I can usually persist with the plan and send my bad attitude packing (but if not, a new day, a new skirt, a trip to town, and a cookie – that's not burnt – go a long way too).

Bible Connection:
A Mother's Persistence Saves Her Son

A woman made a room in her house for Elisha to stay in. In return, Elisha asked God to give her a son, since she'd been unable to have children. God blessed her with a son, but one terrible day he died in her arms at a very young age. The day just kept getting worse when she went to get Elisha, and he was going to send his servant instead of coming himself. But because of the woman's persistent attitude and faith in God, he was convinced to go to her son himself. Elisha prayed for her son and stretched his body next to his several times. The boy opened his eyes, and the woman fell at Elisha's feet in gratitude. (II Kings 4:8-37)

Personal Connection
Role #3: Mother

This woman's hospitable attitude earned Elisha's respect, and her persistence caused her son to be healed. As mothers, let's be persistent in seeking God's plan. Then, after God has led us to a certain course of action, let's follow it through, with faith that He will help us persevere.

 A Welcome Retreat

Prayer to Share (with children): *Help us have a persistent attitude toward the course of action You've mapped out for us.*
Question: Do you have a persistent attitude toward the things the Lord has asked you to do?
Contemporary Music – *Worship* CD:
  Song Title: *"Let It Rain"* – Track 8
Traditional Music – *Ryman Gospel Reunion* CD:
  Song Title: *"I Need You"* – Track 15

Chapter 1: Day 4

Attitude Is a Choice

> I discovered I always have choices
> and sometimes it's only a choice of attitude.
> - Judith M. Knowlton

Every summer, my whole family walked our bean fields together. We'd begin by getting up in the wee hours of the morning and dressing in our "bean walking clothes". When we got to the field, we'd count rows. My dad took eight rows, and the rest of us took four. We'd trudge down the rows, and spray the weeds with Round-up. We would work all day, only breaking for lunch.

We got so dirty from the dust of the fields that our bath water would turn instantly brown when we got into it. We had a hard time getting the dirt off of our skin and out from underneath our fingernails. It really didn't matter though, because we would just get dirty again the next day anyway.

Walking beans sounds like an awful thing to do, doesn't it? But we actually thought it was kind of fun. We packed special lunches, drank pop, sang, and played games while we walked. My dad taught us the names of weeds, and we had contests to see who could shout out the names the fastest. My parents also paid us by the hour, and when we finished all of the fields, we went on a family vacation to celebrate.

We thought walking beans was a family event, as well as an important job that had to be done. Looking back, I'm sure it wasn't something my parents loved to do, but we never knew it. They chose to think positively about it, and their attitude shaped the way we thought about it.

Bible Connection:
A Humble Servant Has a Good Attitude

Jesus told this parable: When your servant comes in from plowing the field, would you tell the servant to sit down and eat? Or, as his master, would you not rather expect him to get your supper first, and wait on you while you eat and drink? After that, would you thank the servant because he did what he was told to do? So you also, when you have done everything you were told to do, should say, *I am an unworthy servant; I have only done my duty.* (Luke 17:7-10)

Personal Connection
Role #4: Teacher

Jesus used this parable to remind us that we were put on this earth to be servants of the Lord. As usual, Jesus doesn't just tell us what we should do, He shows us what we should do by doing it first Himself. Jesus' attitude as a servant of the Lord was humble and respectful. Even when He did tasks as menial as washing people's feet, He didn't complain, draw attention to Himself, or expect appreciation. As teachers of our children, we can model a "no thanks required", humble attitude, and in doing so, begin molding our children - and ourselves - into servants of the Lord.

 ## A Welcome Retreat

Prayer to Share (with children): *Lord, please help us have a good attitude toward work, so we can become Your humble servants.*
Question: Do you model a good attitude toward work that you also expect your children to portray?
Contemporary Music – *Worship* **CD:**
  Song Title: *"Let It Rain"* – Track 8
Traditional Music – *Ryman Gospel Reunion* **CD:**
  Song Title: *"I Need You"* – Track 15

Chapter 1: Day 5
Reflecting on Attitude

Role #1: Christian Woman
What is your attitude toward God when you are having a difficult time in life? When you need to reclaim a reverent attitude, spend some time in nature viewing God's Creation.

Role #2: Wife
Why can it be so difficult to have a helpful attitude toward your husband? Take a moment to ask yourself how you can have a more "willing to help" attitude toward him.

Role #3: Mother
What things has the Lord called you to do in regard to your children? Be persistent in doing them.

Role #4: Teacher
Train your children to respond with a humble and respectful attitude when you ask them to do something. Model this attitude toward work yourself.

A Welcome Retreat

Prayer to Share: *As a Christian woman, a wife, a mother, and a teacher, please help my attitude to be pleasing to You.*

Contemporary Music: *"Let It Rain"*
   Music Connection: Even the earth trembles at the Lord's command because He reigns over all. The Lord's Creation reveals His glory, and your attitude toward Him for even the gift of your life should be reverent and joyful.

Traditional Music: *"I Need You"*
   Music Connection: You need God in your life. Your attitude should reflect total dependence on Him.

Within our family
there was no such thing
as a person
who did not matter.
Second cousins
thrice removed mattered.

- Shirley Abbott

Prepare Your Heart

Prayer:
As a Christian woman, a wife, a mother, and a teacher help my relationships to reflect Your Presence in my life.

Role #1: Christian Woman
Knowing What's Needed Most

Role #2: Wife
Filling Each Other's Needs

Role #3: Mother
Grandma's Legacy of Faith

Role #4: Teacher
A Strong Sense of Security

Contemporary Music Connection:
"Open the Eyes of My Heart"
When you put Jesus in an exalted position in your life, His Presence and glorious light can be seen shining in your relationships.

Traditional Music Connection:
"Old Friends"
God knew there'd be days you'd struggle through, so He sent friends to be with you. He also sent Jesus, and in Him, you have a best friend that is a priceless treasure.

Chapter 2: Day 1

Knowing What's Needed Most

> It is the heart which experiences God, not the reason.
> - Blaise Pascal

<u>My Mother's Eyes</u>
(written by my sister, Cindy, when she was 17 years old)

Ever since I was a little girl
I've looked into my mother's eyes,
searching for her wise answers
to my questions that constantly arise.
When I'm tossed in the troubles of life
her eyes are a guiding light,
I know I can turn to her
for words of comfort and insight.
When I'm excited about my dreams
her eyes sparkle with happiness for me;
she gives me sound assurance
when I wonder what my future will be.
When the world is harsh and cold
I find in her eyes the warmth I need;
she never fails to give me confidence,
her support for me is guaranteed.
Then there are those times
it seems I can face my problems no longer;
Mom hugs me tight and in her eyes
I find a courage that makes me stronger.
And impressed on my mind forever
are the times when her eyes are closed
those times she's saying a prayer for me
because life is tough, she knows.
But Mom's eyes are most beautiful
when I see them filled with tears;
they are tears of overwhelming love
the love she so generously gives.

I cherish her look of love
it is a precious gem I treasure
Her soft, radiating look of love
will shine in my heart forever.

BIBLE CONNECTION:
MARY KNOWS WHAT'S NEEDED MOST

Mary sat at Jesus' feet listening to what He said. But Martha was distracted by all the preparations that had to be made. She came to Jesus and asked Him to tell Mary to help her. "Martha, Martha," Jesus answered, "you are worried and upset about many things, but only one thing is needed. Mary has chosen what is better, and it will not be taken away from her." (Luke 10:38-42)

PERSONAL CONNECTION
ROLE #1: CHRISTIAN WOMAN

Martha was so caught up in her "to do" list, that she failed to do the one thing that was needed most… stop to give Jesus her full attention. In contrast, Mary chose to sit and listen attentively to Him. My mother has always known when to be a "Martha" and when to be a "Mary". As Christian women, let's be willing to put our "to do" lists aside, when listening is the one thing that is needed most.

 A WELCOME RETREAT

Prayer to Share: *Lord, help me to know when to be busy like Martha, and when to be still and listen like Mary.*
Question: Are you so caught up in your "to do" list that you aren't stopping to do what's needed most?
Contemporary Music – *Worship* CD:
 Song Title: *"Open the Eyes of My Heart"* – Track 5
Traditional Music – *Ryman Gospel Reunion* CD:
 Song Title: *"Old Friends"* – Track 23

 ## Chapter 2: Day 2

Filling Each Other's Needs

> When Adam was lonely, God created for him
> not ten friends but one wife.
>   - The Samaritan

I was listening to a Christian radio station when the DJ asked, "Do you think your husband needs you to show him respect, as much as you need him to show you love?" *No way,* I thought. *Rich is too independent to care about respect that much, certainly not like I care about love.* The DJ must have read my mind because he suggested doing a little experiment if I didn't believe respect was that important to my husband.

He said I was supposed to tell my husband, *I've been thinking about all of the ways I respect you,* and then I was supposed to walk away. I decided to give it a try, so when Rich got home, I did the experiment, expecting nothing to happen. However, Rich began following me as I walked away, and he earnestly asked me what I respected about him. He had an intense look about him, and he stared deeply into my eyes. I began to take this more seriously. I spoke slowly and chose my words carefully as I told him he's a hard worker, a good provider, and a loving father.

He stood very still and pondered what I'd said, and then he quietly began to share what he felt he was doing well, and what he felt he was struggling with. Rich isn't very serious, very often, and I couldn't believe how showing him a little respect helped him open up. The DJ was right. Respect is that important to men. Respect means to show consideration for, to admire, to hold a high opinion of, to revere, to value, and to appreciate. I feel all of those things toward Rich, and they are a core part of why I love him.

Love and respect go hand in hand, and they cannot be separated. If we want to feel loved, maybe we need to start by making our husbands feel respected.

BIBLE CONNECTION:
ADAM AND EVE FILL EACH OTHER'S NEEDS

The Lord God said, "It is not good for the man to be alone. I will make a helper suitable for him." So God made a woman from the rib He took out of the man, and He brought her to him. Therefore, a man is to be united with his wife, and they will become one flesh. (Genesis 2:18-24)

PERSONAL CONNECTION
ROLE #2: WIFE

The Lord knew that it was not good for man to be alone, so He gave him one woman. As wives, we need to recognize that we have a role to fill for our husbands that no one else can. Our husbands want our respect, as much as we want their love. Showing respect to our husbands is the first step to achieving true intimacy. Don't hold back any more, share your respect as well as your love with your husband, and it will come back tenfold.

 A WELCOME RETREAT

Prayer to Share (with husband): *Lord, help my husband and I to work together to fill each other's needs.*
Question: Would your husband say you show him you respect him? Would you say your husband shows you he loves you?
Contemporary Music – *Worship* CD:
   Song Title: *"Open the Eyes of My Heart"* – Track 5
Traditional Music – *Ryman Gospel Reunion* CD:
   Song Title: *"Old Friends"* – Track 23

Chapter 2: Day 3

Grandma's Legacy of Faith

> Home wasn't built in a day.
> - Jane Ace

Grandma Mellema married my grandpa when she was very young, and she worked right alongside my grandpa and her sons on the family farm. When my grandpa passed away, she moved to town. Although we lived just down the street, Grandma insisted on scooping her own snow and washing her own car, even when she was eighty years old. No matter how early my dad got up to shovel Grandma's driveway, it was always done before he got there.

Grandma had a definite sweet tooth. Her cupboards were always stocked with lots of treats, and she baked amazing pies. When we went to Grandma's house, we'd drink hot tea, take long hot baths, and feast on home-baked cookies.

Grandma never missed a church service. She went to both the morning and evening services every Sunday… and we did too. Grandma began every meal with prayer… and we did too. Grandma made sure my dad went to Sunday school every week… and we did too. Grandma baked an angel food cake for Jesus' birthday every Christmas… and we still do too.

Before Grandma passed away, we were blessed enough to have the chance to say goodbye. My sister Carrie told Grandma that all of us girls drank hot tea, took hot baths, and loved sweet treats because of her. But most important of all, she told of how Grandma had passed her faith on to our father, who then passed it on to us. Because of this legacy of faith, we would all be able to see her again in eternity. Grandma smiled and passed away soon after.

Bible Connection:
Lois and Eunice's Legacy of Faith

Paul wrote of the legacy of Timothy's faith. He said this faith had first lived in Timothy's Grandmother Lois and then in his mother Eunice. He said that Timothy had known the Holy Scriptures from infancy and could be convinced of his faith because he knew those from whom he'd learned it. (II Timothy 1:15; II Timothy 4:14-15)

Personal Connection
Role #3: Mother

Lois and Eunice knew that the most important thing they could pass on to Timothy was their faith. My grandma knew this as well, and her faith lives on today in each member of my family. As mothers, we can get too busy trying to "build home in a day". Let's remember that the most important legacy we can leave our children is our faith. This faith will give them an eternal home that we'll be able to share with them forever.

 ## A Welcome Retreat

Prayer to Share (with children): *Lord, the best thing I can share with my children is my faith. Please help them to pass their faith on to their children someday too.*

Question: Can your children tell by the things you do that your faith in Jesus is more important than anything else?

Contemporary Music – *Worship* CD:
  Song Title: *"Open the Eyes of My Heart"* – Track 5

Traditional Music – *Ryman Gospel Reunion* CD:
  Song Title: *"Old Friends"* – Track 23

Chapter 2: Day 4
A Strong Sense of Security

> There's a thread that binds all of us together, pull one end of the thread, the strain is felt all down the line.
> - Rosamond Marshall

A wealthy woman was considering the purchase of a bronze buffalo for the hefty price of $3000. It was my first day of work at the Mount Rushmore gallery. The week prior to beginning this college summer job, I'd had four wisdom teeth pulled. There were big, black bruises on my cheeks, and I could hardly imagine someone doing a worse job of selling that buffalo.

Surprisingly, the lady did buy the buffalo. She paid cash and as I counted back her change, she leaned forward and said, "Don't be afraid to get help. He's not worth it, you know." As her husband humped the bronze buffalo out of the store, I mulled over her confusing words. It finally occurred to me that she thought I was being abused.

It was not a good first day at work, and I was 6 hours away from my parents at home. To make things worse, as the day wore on, my gums began to throb. By mid-morning, my mouth was so swollen, I could hardly swallow.

I called my parents, and I garbled my way through my predicament. My dad came right away, making the six-hour drive in record time. He took me to the local hospital, where the doctor told me I had dry sockets. I was given laughing gas during the procedure, so I really don't remember much that happened. However, the one thing that I do remember is hearing my dad's voice calling my name as I woke up. I remember him hugging me, and staying with me until I was strong again. Most of all, I remember that he dropped everything and came, just because I needed him.

Bible Connection:
Jesus, Our Shepherd, Gives Us Security

Jesus told this parable: "I am the good shepherd; I know My sheep and My sheep know Me – just as the Father knows Me and I know the Father – and I lay down My life for the sheep." Jesus calls each sheep by name, and the sheep follow because they know His voice. (John 10:14-16)

Personal Connection
Role #4: Teacher

Jesus takes His role as our Shepherd seriously, and my dad takes his role as a father seriously too. I've always felt a strong sense of security because I've been able to depend on my dad and my Lord. Let's take our role of teaching our children about Jesus seriously. Let's teach them to depend on the Lord, and let's be dependable ourselves too.

   A Welcome Retreat

Prayer to Share (with children): *Jesus, thank you for being so dependable. Help my children to know that I am dependable too.*
Question: Do your children know that you depend on the Lord?
Contemporary Music – *Worship* CD:
  Song Title: *"Open the Eyes of My Heart"* – Track 5
Traditional Music – *Ryman Gospel Reunion* CD:
  Song Title: *"Old Friends"* – Track 23

Chapter 2: Day 5

Reflecting on Meaningful Relationships

Role #1: Christian Woman
Thinking of your average day, would you characterize yourself as more of a "Martha" or a "Mary"? Reflect on the need for balance.

Role #2: Wife
Consider doing the experiment mentioned in the devotional, or at least take time to tell your husband what you respect about him. Pay attention to his response.

Role #3: Mother
When was the last time you told your children what your faith in Jesus means to you? Share it with them today.

Role #4: Teacher
Model dependence on the Lord. Be dependable yourself by being available to your children when they need you.

A Welcome Retreat

Prayer to Share: *As a Christian woman, a wife, a mother, and a teacher, help my relationships to reflect Your Presence in my life.*

Contemporary Music: *"Open the Eyes of My Heart"*
  Music Connection: When you put Jesus in an exalted position in your life, His Presence and glorious light can be seen shining in your relationships.

Traditional Music: *"Old Friends"*
  Music Connection: God knew there'd be days you'd struggle through, so He sent friends to be with you. He also sent Jesus, and in Him, you have a best friend that is a priceless treasure.

For attractive lips,
speak words of kindness.
For lovely eyes,
seek out the good in people.
For a slim figure,
share your food with the hungry.
For beautiful hair,
let a child run his or her fingers
through it once a day.
For poise,
walk with the knowledge
you'll never walk alone.

~ Audrey Hepburn

Prepare Your Heart

Prayer:
As a Christian woman, a wife, a mother, and a teacher, help me focus on the way I appear to You.

Role #1: Christian Woman
Getting Caught Up in Appearances

Role #2: Wife
Attraction That Endures

Role #3: Mother
Attraction to Trouble

Role #4: Teacher
Appearing to Be Perfect

Contemporary Music Connection:
"The Heart of Worship"
Jesus looks past appearances and searches your heart. He wants more than surface beauty; He wants something of a deeper worth.

Traditional Music Connection:
"Goodbye World Goodbye"
When you get caught up in the appearance of things, take time to talk with God and remember this world will not be your home forever.

Chapter 3: Day 1

Getting Caught Up in Appearances

> God's definition of beauty is a lot different
> than the world's. God says that beauty is found
> in a gentle, quiet, and obedient spirit.
> - Heather Whitestone

The time in my life when I was the most caught up in appearances was when I was chosen to compete in a pageant. Pressure to look my best began to mount, and I started running at the track every day. I lost 15 pounds, hi-lighted my hair, and tanned my fair-skinned body to a deep bronze. By the time I actually competed, I just wanted it all to be over. Thankfully, I did not win, and I never had to make an appearance in a beauty pageant again.

Since then, I've had two beautiful babies. Along with each bundle of joy, I've gained some weight, some stretch marks, and some scars. I don't have time to run at the track or tan, but I do try to exercise. Through perseverance, I'm almost back to my pre-pregnancy weight. On most days, I feel fine about the way I look… but, once and awhile, I start to miss looking younger and having a better figure.

There are – and always will be – women who spend most of their lives trying to portray a flawless appearance. However, taking joy in appearance is a fleeting pleasure because it cannot last forever. The most rare beauty can be found in women who have devoted their lives to becoming more like Christ. By that definition, I am more beautiful now than I've ever been in my life, and I will only become more beautiful as I age. That kind of beauty is eternal, and it far surpasses any beauty attainable here on earth.

Bible Connection: Bernice and Agrippa Make an Appearance

King Agrippa and his stunning sister, Bernice, visited the governor who was overseeing Paul's trial. During their stay, they became so intrigued with Paul's case that they decided to attend his trial themselves. The next day, King Agrippa and Bernice dressed in their most beautiful attire and won a lot of attention as they entered the trial. After listening to Paul's account, the King said, "Do you think that in such a short time you can persuade me to be a Christian?" Paul replied that he would pray all who listened to him would become Christians. (Acts 25:13-27; 26:25-31)

Personal Connection
Role #1: Christian Woman

The king and Bernice made the mistake of getting caught up in appearances instead of listening to Paul's compelling testimony. Their regal entrance into the courtroom that day no longer has any impact, but their choice not to become Christians has eternal impact. In contrast, women that live by God's definition of beauty have the opportunity to be beautiful their entire lives, rather than just for fleeting moments. As Christian women, let's embrace growing older as a way to become more beautiful in God's eyes.

A Welcome Retreat

Prayer to Share: *Lord, I want to be beautiful in Your eyes. Help me try not to get caught up in appearances.*
Question: Are you sometimes caught up in appearances?
Contemporary Music – *Worship* CD:
 Song Title: *"The Heart of Worship"* – Track 2
Traditional Music – *Ryman Gospel Reunion* CD:
 Song Title: *"Goodbye World Goodbye"* – Track 3

 ## Chapter 3: Day 2

Attraction That Endures

> Infatuation is when you think that he's as sexy as Robert Redford, as smart as Henry Kissinger, as noble as Ralph Nadar, as funny as Woody Allen, and as athletic as Jimmy Conners. Love is when you realize that he's as sexy as Woody Allen, as smart as Jimmy Conners, as funny as Ralph Nadar, as athletic as Henry Kissinger, and nothing like Robert Redford – but you'll take him anyway.
> - Judith Viorst

When I first met Rich, I remember thinking that I had finally found a man who was mature. There was no "game playing" with Rich. He was a "say it like it is" kind of guy, and that was very attractive to me. I also thought he was handsome and quite a gentleman too. He talked to me for hours, he opened doors for me, and he insisted on paying for all of our dates. After a year together, I knew Rich was the man I wanted to marry.

Throughout our marriage, there have been times the traits I've listed above have not been true. For instance, Rich did not seem very mature to me when he put toilet paper in my shoes. He didn't seem like a "say it like it is" kind of guy when he came home 2 days late from fishing. He wasn't handsome after returning from a four-day hunt without showering. He doesn't have as much time to talk to me anymore, and he doesn't always get the door for me. However, there is one thing I know for sure. Nothing is as attractive to me as my husband. True attraction comes from true love, and true love can only come from *really* knowing someone. Simply put, no other man is as attractive to me as Rich because no other man is my husband.

BIBLE CONNECTION:
HERODIAS' AND HEROD'S ROVING ATTRACTION

Herodias was married to a ruler named Philip, until she met his more powerful brother named Herod. She was so attracted to Herod's power that she divorced Philip to marry Herod instead. John the Baptist told Herod, "It is not lawful for you to have your brother's wife." So Herodias nursed a grudge against John. When Herodias' daughter danced for Herod, he was so attracted to her that he told her he would give her anything she wanted. Herodias told her daughter to ask for the head of John the Baptist, and John was beheaded. (Mark 6:17-29)

PERSONAL CONNECTION
ROLE #2: WIFE

Herodias' attraction to power caused her to marry her husband's brother. Herod's attraction to physical beauty caused him to marry his brother's wife and promise her daughter anything she wanted. It's dangerous to be attracted to a certain trait rather than a certain person. As wives, let's be attracted to the man we married rather than a certain trait that many men could possess. Attraction for our husbands has God's blessing, so it's worth safeguarding.

 A WELCOME RETREAT

Prayer to Share (with husband): *Lord, thank you for the attraction I feel for my husband. No other man compares to him.*
Question: Does your husband know that you're still attracted to him?
Contemporary Music – *Worship* CD:
   Song Title: *"The Heart of Worship"* – Track 2
Traditional Music – *Ryman Gospel Reunion* CD:
   Song Title: *"Goodbye World Goodbye"* – Track 3

Chapter 3: Day 3

Attraction to Trouble

> Experience is a good teacher, but she sends in terrific bills.
> - Minna Antrim

I was 7 years old, and my family was going on a guided horseback ride in the Rocky Mountains. Everyone else in my family had fast, sleek horses that looked as if they could win a race. My horse, which was named Shoofly, looked like movement of any kind would be a challenge.

Shoofly was extremely docile, and she'd led a very predictable life as a workhorse. Since I was so young, the guide chose to break from tradition and use Shoofly as my horse. As we began riding, Shoofly barely moved. Much to my dismay, she and I were soon last in line. By the time the guide looked back, Shoofly had come to a complete halt. I could barely hear the guide as he yelled for me to dig in my heels and yell to get her going, but I gave it my best effort.

At first, Shoofly didn't even blink. But then, she suddenly took off, galloping at a breakneck speed past everyone in the riding party. I held on tightly, and before I knew it, we were in the lead and diving into a river. The water was so deep that Shoofly had to swim, and rapids were looming ahead by the time the guide caught up to us and slung me onto his horse. Shoofly was in a panic as she swam to the other side of the river and headed home, racing back to the workhorse stable.

Shoofly became startled when she began racing ahead into the unknown. After running into trouble, all she could think about was how attractive getting back home sounded.

BIBLE CONNECTION: DINAH'S ATTRACTION TO TROUBLE

Dinah, the only daughter of Jacob and Leah, was attracted to the thrills of a nearby city and went out unattended to visit the women of the land. Shechem, the ruler of the area, was attracted to Dinah and took her for himself. Later, his heart was drawn to her, and he said he loved her. But by then, two of Dinah's brothers were so enraged, that they attacked and killed every man in the city. (Genesis 34:1-25)

PERSONAL CONNECTION
ROLE #3: MOTHER

Dinah, as an only daughter, probably led a predictable life under the very watchful eyes of her many brothers. Going to town unattended must have seemed like an exciting idea, but it had disastrous results. Just like Dinah, our children will want to race ahead into the unknown at times, which may cause them to be inadvertently attracted to trouble. As mothers, it's tough to find a balance between keeping our children at home "in the stables" and letting them "run free" through the mountains of life. We need to try our best to guide them in the right direction, and if they stray, we can pray that they'll head back home to us.

 A WELCOME RETREAT

Prayer to Share (with children): *Lord, help my children to be careful of racing into things they don't know much about.*
Question: Do you recognize which situations attract your children to trouble?
Contemporary Music – *Worship* CD:
  Song Title: *"The Heart of Worship"* – Track 2
Traditional Music – *Ryman Gospel Reunion* CD:
  Song Title: *"Goodbye World Goodbye"* – Track 3

 ## Chapter 3: Day 4
Appearing to Be Perfect

> My father used to play with my brother and me in the yard. Mother would come out and say, "You're tearing up the grass." "We're not raising grass," Dad would reply. "We're raising boys."
> - Harmon Killebrew

Rich was not thinking of our neighbors the day he purchased an old three-wheeler. Looking at the rusted three-wheeler with its chipped paint, crooked handlebars, and torn seat cover, it was tough to imagine it would ever run again. However, Rich can fix almost anything, and he was soon revving it up to take our son Wyatt for a ride. The muffler could be heard many blocks away, and I knew the neighbors wouldn't like it, but Rich and Wyatt were so excited, that I didn't have the heart to stop them.

Almost every day of the fall season, Rich and Wyatt roared down the street past the neighbors. I began longing for winter so the three-wheeler could be put away. When winter came, Rich decided to attach a sled to the back of the three-wheeler, so Wyatt and he could do cookies in the front yard. When spring came, Rich decided to take our two labs along on the rides, so they could get some exercise. When summer came, Rich and Wyatt roared down the street, dogs in tow, to get treats at the local gas station.

I've come to realize that a three-wheeler has a use every season. It's hard sometimes, but the thought *What about the neighbors?* needs to take a backseat when a father/son relationship is at hand. Irreplaceable memories are being made, and that's worth sacrificing a perfect appearance.

BIBLE CONNECTION:
A PHARISEE WORRIES ABOUT APPEARANCES

Jesus told this parable: A Pharisee and a tax collector went to the temple to pray. The Pharisee appeared to be perfect as he stood up and prayed about himself, thanking God that he was not like other men because he fasted and gave a tenth of what he owned to God. But the tax collector asked God to have mercy on him because he was a sinner. Jesus said only the tax collector went home justified by God, for everyone who exalts himself will be humbled, and he who humbles himself will be exalted. (Luke 18:9-14)

PERSONAL CONNECTION
ROLE #4: TEACHER

The Pharisee was so worried about appearing to be perfect that he didn't even accomplish what he went to the temple to do, which was to be justified. The tax collector was less worried about appearances, and because he humbly admitted his sins, he was justified. Sometimes sacrificing a perfect appearance is necessary to do. As teachers of our children, let's stop worrying about appearances. How the Lord sees us is most important, and our appearance will be most perfect when it reflects Him.

 A WELCOME RETREAT

Prayer to Share (with children): *Lord, help us not to be overly worried about appearances; how You see us is most important.*
Question: Do you worry too much about trying to appear to be perfect?
Contemporary Music – *Worship* CD:
  Song Title: *"The Heart of Worship"* – Track 2
Traditional Music – *Ryman Gospel Reunion* CD:
  Song Title: *"Goodbye World Goodbye"* – Track 3

Chapter 3: Day 5

Reflecting on Attraction and Appearance

Role #1: Christian Woman
On a scale of 1 to 5, with 5 being the most, how often do you think about your outward appearance? How about your inward appearance?

Role #2: Wife
When was the last time you told your husband you are attracted to him? Tell him what special things attract you to him and make you want him to be the only man in your life.

Role #3: Mother
What certain people or situations attract your children to trouble? Do your best to educate your children about the danger at hand or remove them from the temptation.

Role #4: Teacher
Teach your children to weigh the importance of a perfect appearance with the importance of being humble.

 A Welcome Retreat

Prayer to Share: *As a Christian woman, a wife, a mother, and a teacher, help me focus on the way I appear to You.*

Contemporary Music: *"The Heart of Worship"*
  Music Connection: Jesus looks past appearances and searches your heart. He wants more than surface beauty; He wants something of a deeper worth.

Traditional Music: *"Goodbye World Goodbye"*
  Music Connection: When you get caught up in the appearance of things, take time to talk with God and remember this world will not be your home forever.

Time isn't a commodity,
something you
pass around like cake.
Time is the substance of life.
When anyone asks you
to give your time,
they're really asking
for a chunk of your life.

~ Antoinette Bosco

Prepare Your Heart

Prayer:
As a Christian woman, a wife, a mother, and a teacher, help me find time for the most important things.

Role #1: Christian Woman
The Pressure of Using Time Wisely

Role #2: Wife
Trying to Be an Excellent Wife

Role #3: Mother
When to Say "Yes" and When to Say "No"

Role #4: Teacher
What Are You Busy Doing?

Contemporary Music Connection:
"The Heart of Worship"
When your life is full of stress, strip away the insignificant things. By making your life all about God, you can focus on what's most important.

Traditional Music Connection:
"Walk Right Out of This Valley"
When you feel short on time, you probably need more time with God. Faithfully spending time with God will help you through the valleys of life.

Chapter 4: Day 1

The Pressure of Using Time Wisely

> You will never "find" time for anything.
> If you want time you must make it.
> - Charles Buxton

I'd taught for 7 years, and I'd just finished my master's degree. I was a busy career woman, and I didn't have time for much else. When I had my first baby, I resolved to make some changes by job sharing with my sister Carrie. At first it seemed like the perfect answer, but it soon became clear we both had to be at the school for many things. After doing plans together, we were spending almost the same amount of time at our jobs as before we job shared.

As I dropped Wyatt off at daycare one morning, he stood at the door and sobbed. His little hands pressed against the glass of the door, reaching out to me. I cried as I drove away, but once I got to work, I focused on my job. Later, as I picked Wyatt up from daycare, I realized I hadn't thought about him one time the entire day, and I felt like the worst mother ever. In that moment of time, I knew I had to make it a priority to be home with Wyatt.

It wasn't easy, and my husband wasn't completely supportive at first, so I worked hard to find part time work I could do from home. First, I tutored students, and then I worked another 3 years at home on my computer, as an on-line tutor for a Christian academy. After that, I quit completely. I have never regretted the decision to be home. Maybe it is not for every woman, but in my case, I know I am a better mother, a better wife, and a happier woman. It is truly one of the best decisions I have ever made.

BIBLE CONNECTION:
LYDIA SPENDS TIME ON IMPORTANT "BUSINESS"

Lydia was a busy career woman who sold valuable and expensive purple cloth. As she listened to Paul share the gospel one day, God opened her heart to respond to his message. After Lydia and all of the members of her household were baptized, she persuaded Paul to stay at her house. Later, after Paul and his friend Silas escaped from falsely being imprisoned, the first place they chose to go was Lydia's house. (Acts 16:14-15, 40)

PERSONAL CONNECTION
ROLE #1: CHRISTIAN WOMAN

Lydia stopped what she was doing to make it a priority to give her heart to God. God revealed that need to her, just as He revealed a need to me on the day I stopped teaching at public school. As Christian women, we need to consider how best to use our time. God may be speaking to you through the pressures in your life. He may be telling you to slow down and consider what's really most important. There will never be more than 24 hours in a day, so we can't expect to find leftover time for the really important things. If we want time, we must make it.

A WELCOME RETREAT

Prayer to Share: *Lord, help me to use my time in a way that You find pleasing. Please reveal how my time on earth will be best served.*

Question: Are you using your time wisely, or are you letting the pressures of life decide how your day is spent?

Contemporary Music – *Worship* CD:
  Song Title: *"The Heart of Worship"* – Track 2

Traditional Music – *Ryman Gospel Reunion* CD:
  Song Title: *"Walk Right Out of This Valley"* – Track 11

Chapter 4: Day 2
Trying to Be an Excellent Wife

> The whole point of getting things done
> is knowing what to leave undone.
> - Lady Stella Reading

I was stressed out and feeling drained when my husband Rich pointed out that I could do a better job of cleaning our hardwood floors. I did not receive his advice very well, probably because I saw the evidence of several past meals stuck to the floor, and I knew he was right. I made a very big show of noisily cleaning the hardwood floors, making sure Rich could notice what a difficult job it was.

I was still angry about it several days later when I told Rich that I was exhausted trying to be an excellent wife. I said I'd gladly clean the hardwood floors until they were spotless if he could tell me one thing I was already doing that I could stop doing instead. He decided he didn't mind if the hardwood floors weren't always clean then.

It had been a few months since we'd had that talk before I was able to admit that my response was not very Christian. Like most women, I think often about the things that I believe are necessary to be an excellent wife. I am constantly rating myself on each thing, and Rich's low rating of my cleaning made me feel like a failure.

I was having one of those "feeling-like-a-failure" moments when it hit me that Rich didn't ask me to be an excellent wife; he just asked me to clean the floor. It has since occurred to me that the things on my "excellent wife" list may not be on Rich's "excellent wife" list. Since that revelation, our hardwood floors are a lot cleaner. We may have something simple for supper on the days I clean the floor, but Rich never seems to complain.

BIBLE CONNECTION:
A WIFE OF NOBLE CHARACTER

Who can find a wife of noble character? She is worth far more than rubies. Her husband has full confidence in her and lacks nothing of value. She brings him good, not harm, all the days of her life…She watches over the affairs of her household and does not eat the bread of idleness. Her children arise and call her blessed; her husband does also, and he praises her. (Proverbs 31:10-12, 27-28)

PERSONAL CONNECTION
ROLE #2: WIFE

Being like the Proverbs 31 woman seems out of reach most days, but being a good wife to our husband is well within our grasp. As wives, let's find out the things that are most important to our husbands. Then, we can try to focus on accomplishing those things first. We may have to let a few other things on our list go, but I think a happy husband is worth the trade off.

 ## A WELCOME RETREAT

Prayer to Share (with husband): *I want to be the best wife I can be. Help my husband to be clear about what he needs from me.*
Question: Do you know what things are most important to your husband regarding your role as his wife?
Contemporary Music – *Worship* CD:
  Song Title: *"The Heart of Worship"* – Track 2
Traditional Music – *Ryman Gospel Reunion* CD:
  Song Title: *"Walk Right Out of This Valley"* – Track 11

Chapter 4: Day 3
When to Say "Yes" and When to Say "No"

> Minutes are worth more than money.
> Spend them wisely.
> - Thomas P. Murphy

Our family lived on a farm, and we seldom drove into town. Every day, my two sisters and I played together, and we came up with lots of fun things to do. We did musicals, complete with dress-up clothes and umbrellas we turned in time to made-up routines.

We played school for hours on end, with Cindy using a very genuine looking chalkboard to give Carrie and I our assignments. We custom built our Barbies their very own dollhouse. We wallpapered cardboard, sewed little curtains, and made authentic-looking furniture out of matchboxes.

When the weather was nice, we played outside with our cats and dog. We built grand grass huts and made the best mud pies ever. We did gymnastics shows on our swing set and balance beam. We rode our bikes up and down the driveway, and when we were tired of that, we got our dolls and brought them outside to play with on the back porch.

My sisters and I played together from sunup to sundown, every single day, and we were each other's best friends. My mother knew the importance of spending time together as a family. Her decision to say "yes" to family time and "no" to other things is the reason all three of us sisters are best friends today. We all have wonderful memories of growing up, and we still love to get together and "play" – whenever and wherever we get the chance.

Bible Connection:
Jochebed Says "Yes" to More Family Time

Amram and Jochebed had 3 children named Miriam, Moses, and Aaron. Aaron was not yet born when Pharaoh ordered all of the Israelite male babies to be killed. Jochebed hid baby Moses for 3 months, but when she could not hide him any more, she put him in a basket in the reeds and sent Miriam to watch over him. When Pharaoh's daughter found him and wanted to keep him, Miriam quickly offered to find a Hebrew woman to nurse Moses. Pharaoh's daughter agreed, and Miriam ran to get her mother to care for him. (Exodus 2:1-10; Numbers 26:59)

Personal Connection
Role #3: Mother

Jochebed risked a lot to keep her family together, but she's living proof that families working together can do a lot for God; her 3 children led all of the Israelites out of Egypt. As mothers, we may find it difficult to keep our family together. When we decide what to say "yes" to, let's make it be for family time more often than not. Then perhaps our children will be "best friends", as well as siblings.

 A Welcome Retreat

Prayer to Share (with children): *Lord, help us spend as much time together as a family as we can. We'll always be glad we did.*

Question: Are you fostering lifelong relationships among your children by saying "yes" to family time more often than not?

Contemporary Music – *Worship* CD:
 Song Title: *"The Heart of Worship"* – Track 2

Traditional Music – *Ryman Gospel Reunion* CD:
 Song Title: *"Walk Right Out of This Valley"* – Track 11

Chapter 4: Day 4

What Are You Busy Doing?

> It is not enough to be busy; so are the ants.
> The question is, *What are we busy about?*
> - Henry David Thoreau

I was attending a Coffee Break Bible study at another church, when another lady and I talked about how neat it would be if we had one at our church. Before we knew it, the word was out, and we were asked to lead a Coffee Break at our church.

I prayed about it, but I didn't feel I was the right person to lead it. Excuses raced through my mind…*I hadn't attended that many Bible studies myself…I had 2 young children…I didn't know Scripture as well as some other women…My husband traveled…I lived out of town… I'd have to direct it, lead a Bible study group, find children's Story Hour teachers and nursery helpers, get supplies, write a budget, pick materials… I CAN'T DO THIS!*

Thankfully, the Lord intervened. I was studying Exodus, and He began pointing out to me that Moses had made excuses too. Even though his excuses were legitimate, God still used him to do amazing things. In my heart I knew that God was asking me to help start Coffee Break. I realized I was making excuses just like Moses, and I knew it was time to stop making excuses and plunge ahead into the unknown.

Now we're getting ready to begin our second year of Coffee Break at our church. Not everything went perfectly the first year, and I made my share of mistakes, but we did have 55 women come. I often think of the saying, *God doesn't call qualified people; He qualifies the people He calls.* I may not have been the most qualified person to direct, but I was one of the people He called.

BIBLE CONNECTION:
INVITED GUESTS ARE TOO BUSY TO COME

Jesus told this parable: A man was preparing a great banquet and invited many guests. He sent his servant to tell the people that they should come, but they all began to make excuses. The first person said he'd just bought a field, another said he'd just bought some oxen, and still another said he'd just gotten married. Then the master ordered his servant to invite the poor, crippled, blind, and lame. He said, "I tell you, not one of those men who were invited will get a taste of my banquet." (Luke 14:16-24)

PERSONAL CONNECTION
ROLE #4: TEACHER

The Lord is inviting you to be a part of His work. He wants and needs your help, instead of your excuses. As teachers of our children, let's model good volunteer choices. If you are saying "no" to volunteer opportunities at church because you are too busy with other worldly things, rethink your choices and help out with something at church today.

A WELCOME RETREAT

Prayer to Share (with children): *Lord, please show each of us how we can help with Your work in our church.*
Question: Are you teaching your children the importance of volunteering in church by setting an example yourself?
Contemporary Music – *Worship* CD:
   Song Title: *"The Heart of Worship"* – Track 2
Traditional Music – *Ryman Gospel Reunion* CD:
   Song Title: *"Walk Right Out of This Valley"* – Track 11

Chapter 4: Day 5

Reflecting on Stress and Pressure

Role #1: Christian Woman
If you were asked what is most important for you to do for the Lord right now, what would you say? Are you taking some of your time each day for that task?

Role #2: Wife
When your husband specifically asks you to do something, try to do it. If you feel you don't have time to do it, rethink your schedule so you can make the time.

Role #3: Mother
How often do your children play with each other compared to how often they play with other friends?

Role #4: Teacher
What are you doing to help in your church right now? If you aren't helping with anything, consider one thing you could do and volunteer for it today.

 A Welcome Retreat

Prayer to Share: *As a Christian woman, a wife, a mother, and a teacher, help me find time for the most important things.*

Contemporary Music: *"The Heart of Worship"*
  Music Connection: When your life is full of stress, strip away the insignificant things. By making your life all about God, you can focus on what's most important.

Traditional Music: *"Walk Right Out of This Valley"*
  Music Connection: When you feel short on time, you probably need more time with God. Faithfully spending time with God will help you through the valleys of life.

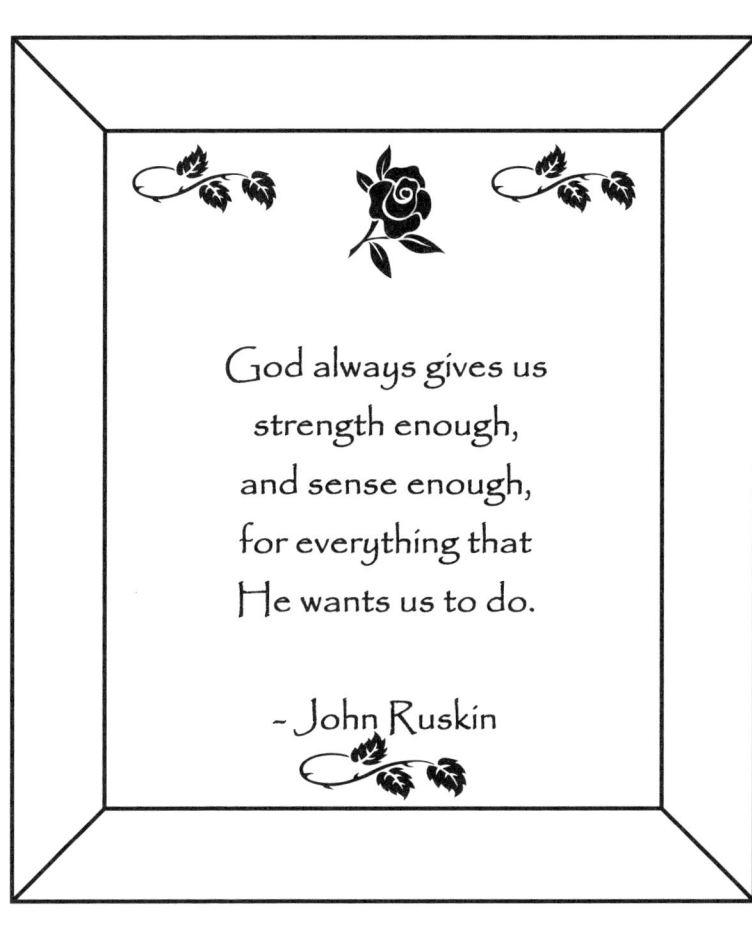

Prepare Your Heart

Prayer:
Please give me the strength of character to be a dedicated Christian woman, wife, mother, and teacher.

Role #1: Christian Woman
Being a Light in Any Situation

Role #2: Wife
Taking a Different Approach

Role #3: Mother
A Strong Faith to Walk the Walk

Role #4: Teacher
A Firm Foundation

Contemporary Music Connection:
"Above All"
Jesus died for your sins because He thought of you above all things. Now, you need to have the strength of character to put Him above all things.

Traditional Music Connection:
"The Lighthouse"
If you follow God's guiding light, you will have the strength to live a Christian life.

 CHAPTER 5: DAY 1

BEING A LIGHT IN ANY SITUATION

> We are told to let our light shine, and if it does, we won't need to tell anybody it does. Lighthouses don't fire cannons to call attention to their shining – they just shine.
> - Dwight L. Moody

Children are often able to see through all of the "talk" to the truth of the matter. Our young son Wyatt has this "telling it like it is" quality in spades. For example, in church, I told Wyatt that he needed to sing because it brought glory to God. When Wyatt said he didn't know the songs, I told him just to sing the parts he knew until he learned to read. After several songs, he turned to Rich and said, "Dad, don't you know any of the songs?"

Later that week, I was singing along with a country music song. There was nothing morally wrong with the song, and Wyatt joined in and sang the chorus. After it was over, Wyatt asked if our singing had brought glory to God. When I said it hadn't, he asked why we'd bothered singing it then.

Recently, we went to a rodeo, and Rich got decked out in his once-a-year cowboy outfit. At the rodeo, Wyatt kept pointing at various cowboys and saying with wonder, "Wow, look at that cowboy!" Rich said, "Hey, what about me?" Wyatt said, "Well, you're not a cowboy, Dad."

We're like that sometimes. We try so hard to look the part of a Christian, only to have our children "tell it like it is" and say, "No, you're not." If our children can't tell we're Christians by the way we live, God won't be able to either.

Bible Connection:
Anna "Tells It Like It Is"

Anna spent her entire lifetime telling people the truth about God. She faithfully worshiped at the temple night and day. She used her time to prophesize, fast, and pray. When Joseph and Mary took baby Jesus to the temple to present Him to the Lord, God sent Anna to them at that very moment. She immediately gave thanks to God and prophesized to everyone that this child would bring about the redemption of Jerusalem. (Luke 2:22, 36-38)

Personal Connection
Role #1: Christian Woman

Anna was a "tell it like it is" person who God chose to help proclaim Jesus as the Christ child. As Christian women, we can aspire to "tell it like it is", like Anna did. We can pray faithfully and look for God's hand in our life. We can also be prepared to share the gospel with fellow sinners. Most importantly, we can be strong enough to let our lights shine so brightly that even a "tell it like it is" person could say with conviction, *Now there is a woman who loves Jesus. There is a woman who is a Christian.*

 A Welcome Retreat

Prayer to Share: *Lord, help people to know I am a Christian before I even tell them I am.*
Question: Can people see you are a Christian without your pointing it out?
Contemporary Music – *Worship* CD:
  Song Title: *"Above All"* – Track 6
Traditional Music – *Ryman Gospel Reunion* CD:
  Song Title: *"The Lighthouse"* – Track 22

Chapter 5: Day 2

Taking a Different Approach

> In the all-important world of family relations, three other words are almost as powerful as the famous "I love you." They are, "Maybe you're right."
> - Oren Arnold

Rich is a "get it done" kind of person, and he's one of the best "fix-it-guys" ever. The problem is our hundred-year-old house has a lot that needs to be "gotten done". Rich works hard to finish many projects, but he never seems to be able to catch up. I'm not always a patient person, and I admit I've often dreamed of secretly calling the local "fix-it-guy" rather than waiting for Rich to find time to do it.

That's why when Rich finished building the back deck, I only did a few weak "oohs" and "ahhs" before asking him when he was going to finish the front steps. He told me he was not motivated to do another job when I couldn't even pause to appreciate the one he'd just finished. I reminded him of how I'd "oohed" and "ahhed", and then I reiterated that the front steps still needed to be fixed. Rich shook his head in disbelief and silently began putting away his tools.

Several months later, I began to wonder if Rich would ever fix the front steps. So, I told him maybe he was right about me not taking time to appreciate the work he had finished. Rich warmed up a little to me and shared that the front steps couldn't be fixed until the cement was laid in the driveway. I'd never thought about that. I guess that's why I'm not the "fix-it-guy". Since then, I've tried to approach Rich with more respect and consideration, and he seems to appreciate it so much more.

BIBLE CONNECTION:
TWO QUEENS HAVE DIFFERENT APPROACHES

King Xerxes was drinking wine when he commanded his wife, Queen Vashti, to display her beauty for his guests. Vashti publicly refused to do this, so Xerxes had her banished. Xerxes then chose a Jew named Esther to be his queen. However, Haman, one of the king's nobles, had a plan to destroy the Jews. When Esther found out, she fasted and prayed. After preparing several banquets for the king, Esther revealed Haman's plan. King Xerxes showed his respect for Esther by having Haman killed. (Esther 1- 7)

PERSONAL CONNECTION
ROLE #2: WIFE

There are many ways wives can approach their husbands with matters of concern. Vashti and Esther had markedly different approaches, and it's easy to see which style worked. As wives, we show strength of character by approaching our husbands with respect and consideration. This may be hard to do at times, but when we forget, saying "maybe you're right" isn't a bad way to mend things either.

 A WELCOME RETREAT

Prayer to Share (with husband): *Lord, help me to approach my husband with respect and consideration.*
Question: Which approach do you most commonly use with your husband – Vashti's or Esther's approach?
Contemporary Music – *Worship* CD:
Song Title: *"Above All"* – Track 6
Traditional Music – *Ryman Gospel Reunion* CD:
Song Title: *"The Lighthouse"* – Track 22

Chapter 5: Day 3

A Strong Faith to Walk the Walk

> There are two things to do about the gospel –
> believe it and behave it.
> - Susannah Wesley

My Grandma Mellema was only 5 feet tall, but she made up in character what she lacked in height. She spent her life quietly serving the Lord, by doing simple things like praying, reading her Bible, and writing in her journal each day. As a little girl, I snuck a peek at her journal and thought *all she writes about is the temperature, weather, church, and people she's visited with – where's the good stuff?* Now, I realize her journal was full of what Grandma considered "the good stuff".

A rose blooming outside my grandma's door on a sunny day reminded her to be in awe of God's Creation. A friend to share a cup of coffee with reminded her to appreciate the company God had given her. A grandchild enjoying a cookie she'd baked gave her reason to remember children are a gift from God. Delivering a meal "to older people who are shut in" reminded her to be thankful for her health (which made sense considering she was in her 80's herself).

My grandma's secret to happiness was not a life free of problems; it was a life full of serving the Lord. God took care of Grandma through hard times, such as marrying young, doing backbreaking farm work, losing her husband to diabetes, and dying of cancer. She did not complain, gossip, or become bitter. She only asked God for enough grace to get through the day, and she trusted Him to provide for her needs. Her faithful walk with the Lord will be an example for my family to follow for generations.

Bible Connection:
Two Women Show Strength of Faith

Mary Magdalene and Mary, the mother of James and John, had a strong faith in God. They trusted Jesus, and they followed Him to Galilee to care for His needs. After He had died, they went to His tomb and watched the stone be rolled across the entrance. After the Sabbath, they took spices to the tomb to anoint Jesus' body. An angel suddenly appeared, asking them to tell the disciples Jesus had risen. On the way to deliver this message, Jesus appeared to them, and they fell at His feet to worship Him. (Matt. 27:56, 61; 28:1; Mark 15:40, 47; 16:1; Luke 24:10; John 19:25)

Personal Connection
Role #3: Mother

These two women believed in Jesus every step of the way. From His walk to the cross to His walk down the road after rising from the dead, they "walked the walk" of faith with Him. My grandma walked that walk of faith too, and as mothers of our children, we need to have the strength of character to do the same. We can't just believe the gospel; we have to behave it. If we do, we hope our children will be right behind us, following in our footsteps to heaven.

 A Welcome Retreat

Prayer to Share (with children): *Lord, help my children and I to have a strong faith in You that can be seen in our every day life.*
Question: Do your children see you "behaving the gospel" on a daily basis?
Contemporary Music – *Worship* CD:
 Song Title: *"Above All"* – Track 6
Traditional Music – *Ryman Gospel Reunion* CD:
 Song Title: *"The Lighthouse"* – Track 22

CHAPTER 5: DAY 4

A FIRM FOUNDATION

> What you teach your own children
> is what you really believe in.
> - Cathy Warner Weatherford

I was in the midst of helping some students who struggled with reading when the teaching announcement came that it was time for the school talent show. As we entered the gym, some scantily clad elementary-aged girls began lip-syncing to a rock song with questionable lyrics. Next, some children performed some karate moves. The act culminated with a boy trying to break a board. Unfortunately, after the fifth try, the board remained unbroken, and the other karate students began laughing at their teammate.

Then, a team of girls wearing clothes even skimpier than the first group of girls danced their way through a very suggestive routine. After more poor attempts at "talent", my ears perked up as a young boy sat down to play Mozart on the piano. I clapped loudly as he finished, but hardly any of the students joined me, and a few of the older ones even booed. A girl playing a violin solo got the same response.

As I trudged back to my classroom, I had the thought that parents would only hear that the school had a great talent show that day. They wouldn't know about the shaky foundation their children were teetering upon after attending that awful talent show, and they wouldn't know their children's reading progress was sacrificed to attend it. It hit me hard that I would not have even wanted my own child to be a part of my class that day, and the idea of homeschooling slowly began to take root in my mind.

BIBLE CONNECTION:
A STRONG OR A WEAK FOUNDATION

Jesus told this parable: Everyone who hears My words and puts them into practice is like a wise man who built his house on the rock. The rain came down, the streams rose, and the winds blew and beat against that house; yet it did not fall because it had its foundation on the rock. But everyone who hears My words and does not put them into practice is like a foolish man who built his house on sand. The rain came down, the streams rose, and the winds blew and beat against that house, and it fell with a great crash. (Matthew 7:24-27)

PERSONAL CONNECTION
ROLE #4: TEACHER

The foundation we give our children will help them to stand or cause them to fall. God did not say that it was up to the schools of this world to train our children. He did not say it was the sole responsibility of the church either. Instead, He gave this responsibility to parents (Proverbs 22:6). The only firm foundation is one grounded upon faith in the Lord. As teachers of our children, let's spend our lives building that foundation, brick by brick, day by day.

 A WELCOME RETREAT

Prayer to Share (with children): *Lord, the most important thing I can ever teach my children is to have faith in You.*
Question: How much time do you spend training your children to know the Lord?
Contemporary Music – *Worship* CD:
  Song Title: *"Above All"* – Track 6
Traditional Music – *Ryman Gospel Reunion* CD:
  Song Title: *"The Lighthouse"* – Track 22

Chapter 5: Day 5
Reflecting on Strength of Character

Role #1: Christian Woman
If your children were to look at you and "tell it like it is", what facets of your life would (or wouldn't) show you are a Christian?

Role #2: Wife
How do you approach your husband with matters of concern? Using respect and consideration means thinking about the timing, tone, and choice of words.

Role #3: Mother
How is your daily walk with the Lord? If your children follow in your footsteps, are they headed in the right direction?

Role #4: Teacher
What are you personally doing to train your children in the Lord? Accept your God-given responsibility and begin helping your children to build that firm foundation today.

A Welcome Retreat

Prayer to Share: *Please give me the strength of character to be a dedicated Christian woman, wife, mother, and teacher.*
Contemporary Music: *"Above All"*
  Music Connection: Jesus died for your sins because He thought of you above all things. Now, you need to have the strength of character to put Him above all things.
Traditional Music: *"The Lighthouse"*
  Music Connection: If you follow God's guiding light, you will have the strength to live a Christian life.

Failure was a part of God's training curriculum for the disciples over one hundred times in the Gospels.
It wasn't until Peter had failed terribly that he was given his greatest responsibility.

~ Roland Niednagel

Prepare Your Heart

Prayer:
As a Christian woman, a wife, a mother, and
a teacher, please forgive me for my many shortcomings.

Role #1: Christian Woman
Mistakes, Shortcomings, and Sins

Role #2: Wife
Overreacting Gets Us Nowhere

Role #3: Mother
Wanting God's Best for Our Children

Role #4: Teacher
Even Superwoman Had Shortcomings

Contemporary Music Connection:
"Purified"
When you feel the weight of your shortcomings, take time to renew your faith in God. True faith has the power to wash away the guilt of your sin and purify you once again.

Traditional Music Connection:
"You and Me Jesus"
When life makes you painfully aware of your imperfections, remember Jesus already knows you're not perfect, yet He is always by your side, choosing to love you in spite of your shortcomings.

Chapter 6: Day 1

Mistakes, Shortcomings, and Sins

> If you have made mistakes, even serious ones, there is always another chance for you. What we call failure is not the falling down, but the staying down.
> - Mary Pickford

Rich and I had just moved into our house, and building a garage and a fence were both somewhere down the middle of our renovations' list. That's why Sage, our chocolate lab, was sleeping outside, chained to a stake, when a black rottweiler came to visit. Sage wasn't interested in him, and she bristled her fur and bit at his heels to let him know it.

The rottweiler visited Sage several more days in a row, and after he had spent several nights at the animal shelter, things seemed under control…until one day when I heard a loud clanking sound coming down the street. It was the rottweiler dragging his chain, with the stake still attached to it. As I dialed animal control, I watched for Sage to begin her "ritual of the rottweiler turndown". Only this time, she pranced toward him in a welcoming sort of way. She sashayed before him, flipping her tail to and fro, and several months later, Sage was the mother of 12 black puppies.

Sometimes, I think Satan can be like that rottweiler because he keeps "doggedly" trying to pursue us. Like Sage, we may resist at first, but over time, we start to weaken. It takes a strong faith (or a fence in Sage's case) to stop us from making sinful mistakes. When we recognize our shortcomings and see that small "mistakes" have piled up into big "sins", we can confess our sins and pray for God's forgiveness. A fresh start is possible with God by our side.

BIBLE CONNECTION:
BATHSHEBA'S BATH RESULTS IN SIN

King David was walking on the roof of his palace when he saw a very beautiful woman bathing on her rooftop. His messengers told him she was Bathsheba, the wife of one of his soldiers. David slept with her anyway, and she became pregnant with his child. To cover up his sin, David had her husband killed by putting him in the front line of the battle. After Bathsheba had mourned her husband's death, David brought her to his house, and she became his wife. But the thing David had done displeased the Lord, and the son born to him became ill and died. (II Samuel 11:2-27; 12:14-19)

PERSONAL CONNECTION
ROLE #1: CHRISTIAN WOMAN

David's shortcoming for lusting after beautiful women like Bathsheba caused him to make a mistake that turned into a sin. Our shortcomings can cause us to make mistakes too. As Christian women, we need to be brave enough to admit when we've made a mistake. We need to realize that the shortcoming is not in making the mistake; it's in covering it up. All of us are sinful and will "fall down", but it's when we "stay down", that Satan has won the pursuit.

 A WELCOME RETREAT

Prayer to Share: *Lord, please help me to recognize the difference between my shortcomings and my sins.*
Question: Do you label some of your mistakes as "shortcomings", when they should be labeled as "sins"?
Contemporary Music – *Worship* CD:
  Song Title: *"Purified"* – Track 12
Traditional Music – *Ryman Gospel Reunion* CD:
  Song Title: *"You and Me Jesus"* – Track 5

Chapter 6: Day 2
Overreacting Gets Us Nowhere

> Husbands are awkward things to deal with; even keeping them in hot water will not make them tender.
> - Mary Buckley

The hotel had over 50 different fantasy suite themes, and I wanted to pick the perfect suite for one of the nights of our honeymoon. Rich was less enthused about the idea, so I passed on the cupid and Cinderella suites and settled for the log cabin one instead. The brochure showed a bearskin rug, a built-in fireplace, and a hot tub sunk in the floor of a forest-like setting. Everything appeared to be decorated log cabin style, and I knew it was going to be just perfect.

When we arrived at the suite, we could hardly believe our eyes. There were huge, fake-looking deer all over the walls, and there were more unsightly deer on the bedspread. It was a cracker box of a room, and there was no walking space along the side of the bed. To get into the bed, we had to leap through a rusty screen door opening between the hot tub area and the bedroom. Rich pointed out that at least it had a hot tub. However, when we turned on the jets, dirt shot out, making the water a dirty brown.

I cried and complained that this was NOT a "fantasy suite". Rich was more frustrated with me than with the room, but he still met with the manager and got half of our money back. Blessedly, God helped me realize I was overreacting, and I was able to readjust my thinking. I have to admit I am still prone to overreacting, but if I realize it, I remind myself I have a choice to respond in a more rational way, and I depend on God to help me adjust my thinking.

BIBLE CONNECTION:
THE SHORTAGE OF WINE AT A WEDDING

Mary, Jesus, and the disciples were attending a wedding when the wine ran out. Mary could have overreacted, but she simply told Jesus there was no more wine, and she instructed the servants to do whatever Jesus wanted. Jesus took control and told the servants to fill six stone jars with water. Then He had the servants take some of it to the master of the banquet to taste. The master of the banquet did not know where it had come from, but he told the bridegroom, "People usually serve the best wine first, but you have saved the best until now." He didn't even realize that Jesus had turned the water into wine. (John 2:1-10)

PERSONAL CONNECTION
ROLE #2: WIFE

In Jesus' day, running out of wine at a wedding was considered to be very inhospitable. Mary could have overreacted, but she chose to turn the problem over to Jesus. In His capable hands, the problem was quickly solved. As wives, when we find ourselves in the middle of overreacting, we should turn our problem over to Jesus, and then depend on Him to help us adjust our thinking.

 A WELCOME RETREAT

Prayer to Share (with husband): *Lord, please help me know when I'm overreacting, so I can choose to be more rational instead.*
Question: Does overreacting really help you and your husband come to a peaceful agreement?
Contemporary Music – *Worship* CD:
   Song Title: *"Purified"* – Track 12
Traditional Music – *Ryman Gospel Reunion* CD:
   Song Title: *"You and Me Jesus"* – Track 5

Chapter 6: Day 3

Wanting God's Best for Our Children

> Failure is an event, never a person.
> - William D. Brown

I was a freshman in high school at my first basketball camp, and I was so excited to be there. I hoped to impress my coach as much as my sister had when she'd played basketball for him, so I jumped as high as I could to get the first rebound. Though I came down with the ball, I also came down wrong on my ankle. It immediately began to swell to twice its size, and it became clear I would not be able to participate in the weeklong basketball camp.

I was crushed, and I told my parents they might as well try to get the $60 camp fee back. My dad surprised me by saying that the camp registration had said there would be no refunds, and I'd just have to make the best of it and learn as much as I could from sitting on the sidelines. Several days later, another girl sprained her ankle. As I watched her parents haggle with the coach to get their money back, I was so glad that my dad had shown more respect.

Throughout my years of playing basketball, many situations such as this arose. I watched parent after parent head into the coach's office to give him their "expert" advice on how things should be done. Before long, the daughters of those parents began giving our coach their "expert" advice too, and the chain of command broke down. My parents respected our coach because his position of authority commanded respect. As a player on my coach's team, I knew his position outranked mine. I followed my parents' lead, and I never had "expert" advice for my coach.

BIBLE CONNECTION:
A MOTHER MAKES A SELFISH REQUEST

The mother of James and John asked Jesus if her two sons could sit at His right and left hand in His kingdom. Jesus told her that she didn't know what she was asking and that this privilege was not for Him to grant. Those places already belonged to whomever they had been prepared for by the Father. Jesus further explained that just as He did not come to earth to be served, but to serve, likewise, whoever wants to be great must be a servant, and whoever wants to be first must be last. (Matthew 20:20-27)

PERSONAL CONNECTION
ROLE #3: MOTHER

This mother's sons were devoted disciples, and she wanted them to receive the credit she thought they deserved. Jesus gently reprimanded her by paying respect to His Father's authority and reminding her that the more appropriate behavior was to be like a servant. As mothers, we naturally want the best for our children. But, the next time we're crossing that line between "wanting the best" and "unfairly forcing the best", let's remember Jesus' advice to this woman and choose to be like a servant instead.

 A WELCOME RETREAT

Prayer to Share (with children): *Lord, help us to remember that showing respect is a necessary quality of a good servant.*
Question: Does wanting the best for your children cause you to do or say things that might be disrespectful?
Contemporary Music – *Worship* CD:
 Song Title: *"Purified"* – Track 12
Traditional Music – *Ryman Gospel Reunion* CD:
 Song Title: *"You and Me Jesus"* – Track 5

Chapter 6: Day 4

Even Superwoman Had Shortcomings

> It is not success that God rewards
> but faithfulness in doing His will.
> - Anonymous

Like most women today, I wanted to have it all. I was going to be Superwoman and do everything just right in my life. I was going to be the perfect wife, career woman, mother, and daughter – sister – granddaughter – friend - daughter-in-law…and oh yes, a strong Christian woman too. This "have it all" plan included getting my master's degree, since that would help me excel at my career.

I took classes during nights, weekends, and summers while still teaching full time. I rushed at a breakneck pace to get my master's degree in two years. I drank 3-4 cans of pop a day, gulped down Slim Fast for lunch, and never saw my husband. It was not a healthy way of living, and in the end I was frustrated because I could see that while I was going to be able to "have it all" in my career, I was not going to be able to "have it all" in the other areas of my life.

Somewhere along the line I fell for the fallacy that I could be Superwoman – probably since that's the way I pictured women as being successful. While I was getting my master's degree, I figured out a little secret: *I can't excel at everything and still have time for God.* Like many women, I was racing through life with blinders on, chasing that elusive dream of "having it all". In the meantime, I was missing the one thing I needed to "have it all", which is faith in Jesus and personal time spent with Him. We are all struggling through spiritual battles every day. Against an adversary as cunning as Satan, we don't have a chance of winning those battles – unless we have the Lord by our side.

BIBLE CONNECTION:
BEING PREPARED GOING INTO BATTLE

Jesus told this parable: If a king is about to go to war against another king, won't he first consider whether his ten thousand men can oppose the one coming against him with twenty thousand? If he is not able, he will send a delegation while the other is still a long way off and ask for terms of peace. In the same way, any of you who do not give up everything you have cannot be my disciple. (Luke 14:31-33)

PERSONAL CONNECTION
ROLE #4: TEACHER

Most of us are a long way off from giving up everything for the Lord. However, we can begin teaching our children discipleship by showing them that time spent on perfecting a Superwoman (or Superman) image could be time better spent trying to become a "super disciple". Perhaps the best way of teaching this would be to trade in our own Superwoman capes for more faith and more time spent with God. That's the best way to be a "super woman" for God.

 A WELCOME RETREAT

Prayer to Share (with children): *Lord, help us to remember that we cannot excel at everything and still have time for You.*
Question: Are you ready to trade in your Superwoman cape and be a "super woman" for God instead?
Contemporary Music – *Worship* CD:
  Song Title: *"Purified"* – Track 12
Traditional Music – *Ryman Gospel Reunion* CD:
  Song Title: *"You and Me Jesus"* – Track 5

Chapter 6: Day 5
Reflecting on Shortcomings

Role #1: Christian Woman
What is your greatest shortcoming? Is that shortcoming causing you to sin? If so, what needs to change?

Role #2: Wife
In regard to your husband, which things do you habitually overreact to? Admit these to your husband, apologize, and strive to be more rational the next time.

Role #3: Mother
Take time to understand the difference between wanting the best for your children and unfairly forcing the best.

Role #4: Teacher
Are you still trying to be Superwoman? Consider the harm that image may do to your children's expectations of themselves and become a "super woman" for God instead.

A Welcome Retreat

Prayer to Share: *As a Christian woman, a wife, a mother, and a teacher, please forgive me for my many shortcomings.*

Contemporary Music: *"Purified"*
  Music Connection: When you feel the weight of your shortcomings, take time to renew your faith in God. True faith has the power to wash away the guilt of your sin and purify you once again.

Traditional Music: *"You and Me Jesus"*
  Music Connection: When life makes you painfully aware of your imperfections, remember Jesus already knows you're not perfect, yet He is always by your side, choosing to love you in spite of your shortcomings.

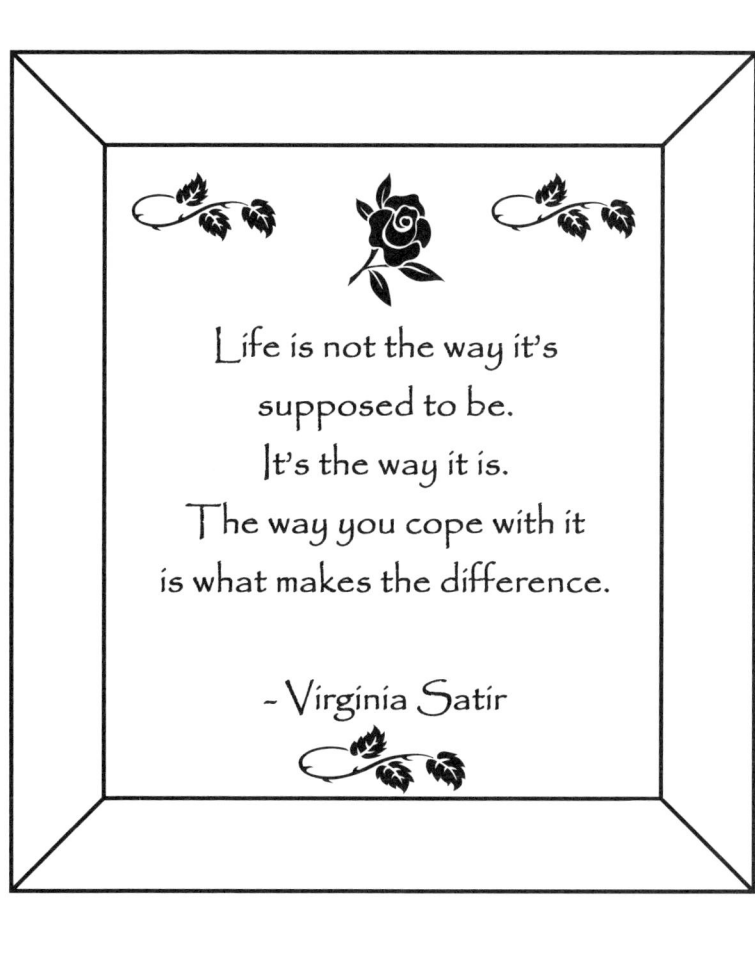

Life is not the way it's
supposed to be.
It's the way it is.
The way you cope with it
is what makes the difference.

- Virginia Satir

Prepare Your Heart

Prayer:
As a Christian woman, a wife, a mother, and a teacher, help me to know which differences really matter.

Role #1: Christian Woman
We're Not So Different After All

Role #2: Wife
Different Ways of Thinking

Role #3: Mother
Differences in Children

Role #4: Teacher
Being Different vs. Fitting In

Contemporary Music Connection:
"Turn Your Eyes Upon Jesus"
When you focus on Jesus, the unimportant things of this world will fade away, and the Lord will make clear which differences really matter.

Traditional Music Connection:
"We'll Understand It Better By and By"
God leads people to Him in many different ways. Every person's spiritual journey will be unique, and someday you will understand why.

Chapter 7: Day 1

We're Not So Different After All

> To understand another human being you must
> gain some insight into the conditions
> which made him what he is.
> - Margaret Bourke-White

I was 9 weeks pregnant with our first baby, and we were all on a family vacation. Before long, I began having painful cramps. I called my doctor and spoke with the head nurse on the phone. After I described my symptoms, she told me in a very businesslike manner that I was probably having a miscarriage. She said I could put my feet up and drink lots of fluids, but the chances of reversing the miscarriage were slim. She matter-of-factly said she had to go unless I had any questions, but I was too devastated to speak.

The nurse was right. It was a miscarriage, and I was not able to stop it. I remember thinking how different she and I were, and that if she had any idea how devastating a miscarriage was, she would not have responded so coldly.

Several months later, I saw the nurse I'd spoken to. When I awkwardly tried to make small talk about how tan she looked, she said she and her husband had just gotten back from a special vacation. After her many miscarriages, she and her husband had decided to take a trip each year to help ease the void they feel about not having any children.

I'd judged her to be uncaring and different from me, but she'd been through the same pain I had. As she's watched me have two babies now, I see the pain behind her indifference, and I think to myself, *we're not so different after all*.

Bible Connection:
A Woman Shows David's Not So Different

King David's heart longed for his estranged son, Absalom, but he'd banished him for killing his other son. A wise woman came to tell David a story. She said her two sons fought, and one killed the other. Her whole clan wanted to kill the remaining son as a punishment. David told her he would not allow her remaining son to be harmed. The woman said, "Why then, has the king not brought back his own banished son?" David realized his own situation was not so different from this story, and he asked for Absalom to be brought back. (2 Samuel 14:1-21)

Personal Connection
Role #1: Christian Woman

David made a judgment about how this woman should react to her hypothetical situation, and he ended up realizing that his situation was not that different from the one she had described. As Christian women, let's not immediately judge people to be different from us. Once we have some insight into their lives, we may realize we're not so different after all.

 A Welcome Retreat

Prayer to Share: *Lord, please help me to remember to stop judging others because they seem different from me.*
Question: Are you quick to judge others that seem different from you?
Contemporary Music – *Worship* CD:
  Song Title: *"Turn Your Eyes Upon Jesus"* – Track 4
Traditional Music – *Ryman Gospel Reunion* CD:
  Song Title: *"We'll Understand It Better By and By"* – Track 6

Chapter 7: Day 2
Different Ways of Thinking

> The goal in marriage is not to think alike,
> but to think together.
> - Robert C. Dodds

Lucy was our four-pound Pomeranian puppy. Although she was very tiny, she had a way of making her presence known. Lucy loved to bark at the top of her little lungs, and she delighted in jumping off of the couch and racing around in circles whenever cars drove by. Lucy also easily became jealous, and if Rich and I were sitting on the couch, she would force herself between us. In the morning, Lucy grunted angrily, as she squeezed between Rich and I, and peered into our eyes.

Lucy had a feisty temper, and she immediately urinated on the carpet if we told her something was a "no-no". If we put her in her kennel, she gnashed her teeth and repeatedly barked in a low snarling sort of way.

After we had our baby, Lucy barked outside his door and woke him up during naps. She urinated under his crib and knocked him over when he tried to crawl. I had a constant headache when Rich said the logical thing to do was find Lucy a new home. I thought that was heartless and wouldn't even consider it at first.

However, several months later, I followed his advice. Weeks later, I called to check on Lucy. Her new owner said *Lucy is great, and...* I couldn't hear the rest because there was so much barking going on. I hung up the phone with a slight headache, and I knew we'd done the right thing.

BIBLE CONNECTION: ZECHARIAH AND ELIZABETH THINK DIFFERENTLY

When Zechariah went into the temple, an angel told him that Elizabeth would bear him a son. Zechariah responded logically by asking how he could be sure, since he and his wife were very old. The angel told him he'd be made silent because he did not believe his news. In contrast, when Elizabeth became pregnant she responded emotionally by saying, "The Lord has done this for me." (Luke 1:6-25)

PERSONAL CONNECTION
ROLE #2: WIFE

God created men and women to think in different ways. Men often think in terms of logic, and women often think in terms of emotions. Zechariah first responded logically because Elizabeth was barren, and Elizabeth first responded emotionally because of her faith. In their situation, Elizabeth's emotional response was the better one. In our decision about Lucy, Rich's logical response was the better one. As wives, let's first listen to our husband's logical response and weigh its merit before giving our emotional response. Different situations require different responses, and sometimes the logical response will be the better one.

 A WELCOME RETREAT

Prayer to Share (with husband): *Lord, when my husband and I think differently, help us consider each other's perspective.*
Question: Do you see that your husband's logical response is sometimes better than your emotional response?
Contemporary Music – *Worship* CD:
  Song Title: *"Turn Your Eyes Upon Jesus"* – Track 4
Traditional Music – *Ryman Gospel Reunion* CD:
  Song Title: *"We'll Understand It Better By and By"* – Track 6

Chapter 7: Day 3

Differences in Children

> The beauty of "spacing" children many years apart lies in the fact that parents have time to learn the mistakes that were made with the older ones – which permits them to make exactly the opposite mistakes with the younger ones.
> - Sydney J. Harris

The first time I vacuumed in front of Wyatt, he burst into tears and looked at the vacuum as if it was going to swallow him up. When I vacuumed in front of our second son, Riley, he squealed with delight and began crawling as fast as he could toward the vacuum to investigate.

At Wyatt's first birthday party, he heartily shoved big hunks of his cake into his mouth, making a real mess and loving it. At Riley's first birthday party, he was so bothered by the frosting sticking to his fingers that he began sobbing and trying to shake it off. As soon as Wyatt could talk, he began pushing me away when I hugged him, saying, "Too much, Mama". However, Riley's little arms are always reaching out for a hug, and he can hardly get close enough.

Wyatt and Riley have differences, but they also have similarities. They both think our lab, Sage, moves way too fast for comfort. They both thought it was neat to tear down the wallpaper in their rooms, and they both love to take bubble baths. They both have big blue eyes, and smiles that light up the room. Most importantly, they both have our love as parents, and that love is not based upon a set of traits that makes one of them better than the other, just because they are different.

BIBLE CONNECTION:
ISAAC AND REBEKAH FAVOR DIFFERENT SONS

Isaac and Rebekah had twin boys named Esau and Jacob. The boys grew up, and Esau became a skillful hunter, a man of the open country, while Jacob was a quiet man, staying among the tents. Isaac, who had a taste for wild game, loved Esau, but Rebekah loved Jacob. When Isaac was old and could no longer see, he called for Esau to give him his blessing. But, Rebekah told Jacob to pose as Esau, so he could have the blessing instead. (Genesis 25:27-28; 27:1-10)

PERSONAL CONNECTION
ROLE #3: MOTHER

Isaac loved Esau best, and Rebekah loved Jacob best. Each of them probably saw more of themselves in the child they seemed to prefer. This is a recipe for a parenting disaster because it makes certain personality traits be the deciding condition for love. We may have one child we see more of ourselves in, but that doesn't mean we should love them more. As mothers, let's appreciate the differences in our children and focus on loving them the same. Then, just maybe they'll do the same for us as parents and love us equally as well.

 A WELCOME RETREAT

Prayer to Share (with children): *Lord, I love each of my children equally, and I'm so glad they are not all exactly alike.*
Question: Do you unintentionally relate better to one of your children because he/she is more like you?
Contemporary Music – *Worship* CD:
  Song Title: *"Turn Your Eyes Upon Jesus"* – Track 4
Traditional Music – *Ryman Gospel Reunion* CD:
  Song Title: *"We'll Understand It Better By and By"* – Track 6

Chapter 7: Day 4

Being Different vs. Fitting In

> We need to teach the next generation of children from day one that they are responsible for their lives.
> - Elisabeth Kubler-Ross

Amy and I were friends from the time that we were little kids. In high school, our relationship began to change. Amy was a strong and mature Christian girl, and I was still searching. I wanted to fit in with my peers and get along with everyone, and Amy had a strong faith that seemed to naturally set her apart. During high school, we had fun together in plays, musicals, and church events, but we gradually grew apart as we made different choices.

If I could go back and do things over again, I would choose to be different rather than to fit in. Amy was always true to her faith, and she can look back at that time in her life and feel good about the decisions she made. I would love to be able to do the same, but many memories from that time in my life bring back regrets and guilt.

Amy is married now, and she and her husband do missionary work in Bangladesh. Each month, I receive a letter explaining the work that Amy and her husband are doing. I know that God was preparing Amy for the great things she is doing today way back when we were in high school. I wasn't prepared to be different for God then, but I am now. I finally understand something Amy understood a long time ago; being a Christian requires some different behaviors, sometimes at the cost of "fitting in". Being prepared for this not only helps us do God's work now, but it also makes us ready for when Christ will come again.

BIBLE CONNECTION:
BEING DIFFERENT BY BEING JESUS' DISCIPLES

Jesus told this parable: I am the vine, and you are the branches. If a man remains in Me and I in him, he will bear much fruit. Apart from Me, you can do nothing. If you are apart from Me, you will be like a cut off branch that is thrown away and left to wither. However, if you remain in Me, and My words remain in you, ask whatever you wish, and it will be given to you. This is to My Father's glory, that you bear much fruit, by showing yourselves to be My disciples. (John 15:5-8)

PERSONAL CONNECTION
ROLE #4: TEACHER

When we are disciples for Jesus, our lives are fruitful because we bring the Father glory. When we are separate from Jesus, our lives are fruitless because we can do nothing apart from God. As teachers of our children, let's prepare them to bear fruit by training them to be God's disciples. Let's help them understand that bringing glory to God allows them to remain close to Him. Most importantly, let's teach them that "fitting in" in our world, is not nearly as important as being prepared for eternity.

 A WELCOME RETREAT

Prayer to Share (with children): *Help my children to know that it's more important to be prepared for eternity than to "fit in".*
Question: Do your children know that because they are Christians it is a natural thing to not always "fit in"?
Contemporary Music – *Worship* CD:
  Song Title: *"Turn Your Eyes Upon Jesus"* – Track 4
Traditional Music – *Ryman Gospel Reunion* CD:
  Song Title: *"We'll Understand It Better By and By"* – Track 6

Chapter 7: Day 5
Reflecting on Differences

Role #1: Christian Woman
Have you ever been judged by someone because they thought you were different? Consider how that felt and try not to misjudge others in the same way.

Role #2: Wife
When your husband responds logically to an issue you find emotional, try saying, "Thanks for your input, and I'll consider what you've said." Then, revisit the issue later.

Role #3: Mother
Is there one of your children you see more of yourself in? How does that effect the way you show love to that child in comparison to the rest of your children?

Role #4: Teacher
Talk with your children about being prepared to be different like Christ rather than just trying to "fit in".

A Welcome Retreat

Prayer to Share: *As a Christian woman, a wife, a mother, and a teacher, help me to know which differences really matter.*

Contemporary Music: *"Turn Your Eyes Upon Jesus"*
  Music Connection: When you focus on Jesus, the unimportant things of this world will fade away, and the Lord will make clear which differences really matter.

Traditional Music: *"We'll Understand It Better By and By"*
  Music Connection: God leads people to Him in many different ways. Every person's spiritual journey will be unique, and someday you will understand why.

Prepare Your Heart

Prayer:
As a Christian woman, a wife, a mother, and a teacher, help me to stand strong against jealousy, envy, and greed.

Role #1: Christian Woman
Jealousy, Envy, and Greed

Role #2: Wife
Jealous of His Interests

Role #3: Mother
Jealous of "Dad Being the Favorite"

Role #4: Teacher
The Cost of Jealousy and Greed

Contemporary Music Connection:
"Above All"
All of the wealth and the wonders of the world cannot compare to the sacrifice Jesus made for you. There is no reason to be jealous, envious, or greedy about earthly things.

Traditional Music Connection:
"Wait'll You See My Brand New Home"
When you begin to covet the things of this world, remember that your heavenly Father is building you a brand new home that is more beautiful and rare than anything here on earth.

Chapter 8: Day 1

Jealousy, Envy, and Greed

> Envy is the art of counting the other
> fellow's blessings instead of your own.
> - Harold Coffin

Our two-story white house was built in 1903. I fell in love with its pocket doors, 10 foot ceilings, original woodwork, and view of open, rolling hills. Although many repairs were needed, I was excited to make this house our home.

We've worked hard on our house over the past five years. We've laid hardwood floor, and we've stained and varnished all of the wood in the house. We've painted and wallpapered each room, added a new furnace and windows, sided and shingled the house, built a garage, replaced the old porch, and fenced in the backyard. We've done almost all of the work ourselves, with some help from our families.

We haven't been the only busy people in our neighborhood. The farmland that provided our view of open, rolling hills was sold, and a housing development began emerging overnight. Each summer that we've worked on repairing our old house, we've seen at least ten new houses built around us. The houses are beautiful, the landscaping flawless, and the neighborhood affluent. Our 1903 house does not look like it belongs here anymore.

I've caught myself enviously gazing out the window at the neat rows of beautiful homes, wishing we could afford to build a new house ourselves. Then, I look around our house, and I remember each part of it coming to life. I remember the hard work and sweat that went into making this house a home, and I turn away from that window of jealousy, choosing to be happy with what I have instead.

BIBLE CONNECTION: JEZEBEL'S JEALOUSY, ENVY, AND GREED

Near Ahab and Jezebel's palace was a beautiful vineyard. Ahab desired this vineyard, but the owner refused to sell it. When Ahab became sullen and angry, Jezebel said, "…Cheer up. I'll get you the vineyard." So Jezebel had the vineyard's owner stoned on false charges of blasphemy. After Ahab and Jezebel took possession of the vineyard, the prophet Elijah told them that dogs would devour them because of their deceit. (I Kings 21:1-23)

PERSONAL CONNECTION
ROLE #1: CHRISTIAN WOMAN

Ahab and Jezebel probably enviously gazed out their window at their neighbor's property, just as I have. Jealousy and greed made them obsessed with owning the vineyard, at all costs. As Christian women, let's count our blessings and be happy with what we have rather than counting others' blessings. Since the Lord has full ownership of all that we have, there's no need to compare ourselves to others. We must know that God has given us all that we need.

A WELCOME RETREAT

Prayer to Share: *Lord, I will choose to be happy with what I have, because I know that You have given me all that I need.*
Question: Are you jealous of others' blessings?
Contemporary Music – *Worship* CD:
  Song Title: *"Above All"* – Track 6
Traditional Music – *Ryman Gospel Reunion* CD:
  Song Title: *"Wait'll You See My Brand New Home"*–Track 19

Chapter 8: Day 2

Jealous of His Interests

> Jealousy sees things always with magnifying glasses that make little things large.
> - Cervantes

When looking through a magnifying glass, all that can be seen is one small part of the big picture. Jealousy is like a magnifying glass, because it focuses on one thing. Every marriage has shades of jealousy, and my biggest source of jealousy is my husband's interest in fishing and hunting.

When I'm looking through my "jealousy magnifying glasses", I see that Rich loves planning his fishing and hunting trips, but he doesn't like making plans to go away with me. When I look at the big picture, I see that Rich feels comfortable planning fishing and hunting trips because that's the way he vacationed growing up.

Through jealous eyes, I see Rich's lack of excitement about the things we've done together. I see how he tells fishing or hunting stories with total exhilaration. When I look at the big picture, I realize that talking about fishing and hunting is just easier for him because he's a man.

With envy, I look at pictures Rich took during his fishing and hunting trips, and I see that Rich rarely takes pictures at birthdays and other occasions. When I look at the big picture, I realize that he's usually busy doing other helpful things at these events so I can take the pictures I want.

Rich has always been an outdoorsman, and I wouldn't want him to give that up. When I look at the big picture, I realize that I don't have to feel threatened by Rich's outside interests, because his greatest interest is still his family.

Bible Connection: Jealousy Between Rachel and Jacob

Jacob was married to both Leah and Rachel, but Jacob loved Rachel more than Leah, so the Lord allowed Leah to give birth to a son. When Rachel was not bearing Jacob any children, she became jealous of Leah and said to Jacob, "Give me children, or I'll die!" Jacob became angry with her and said, "Am I in the place of God, who has kept you from having children?" (Genesis 29:30-31; 30:1-2)

Personal Connection
Role #2: Wife

When Rachel looked through her jealousy magnifying glasses, all she could see was that Leah had children with Jacob first. Later, Rachel also had children, but she was still jealous of Leah for having more children. If Rachel had looked at the big picture, she would have seen that Jacob loved her more than Leah anyway. As wives, let's throw out our jealousy magnifying glasses and look at the big picture instead. It could save us years of envy and heartache, and it could stop jealousy from ruling our lives.

A Welcome Retreat

Prayer to Share (with husband): *Lord, when I'm feeling jealous, help me look at the big picture of our marriage before I react.*
Question: How does jealousy affect your marriage?
Contemporary Music – *Worship* CD:
  Song Title: *"Above All"* – Track 6
Traditional Music – *Ryman Gospel Reunion* CD:
  Song Title: *"Wait'll You See My Brand New Home"* –Track 19

Chapter 8: Day 3

Jealous of "Dad Being the Favorite"

> He can climb the highest mountain or swim the biggest ocean. He can fly the fastest plane and fight the strongest tiger. My father can do anything! But most of the time he just carries out the garbage.
> - Anonymous (eight-year-old)

A child can love their father so much, that everything he does (even taking out the garbage) seems heroic. Heroic fathers can inspire their children in countless ways. Seeing my dad as a hero inspired me to write this poem.

<u>To Be A Mirror Image of My Father</u>
(I wrote this for my dad when I was 29 years old)

Strong Hands…
Not afraid of hard work
Never seeming to tire
Gentle enough to hold you
When you don't live up to what you've aspired

Humble enough to fold in prayer
Reaching out in times of need
Sharing the gift of eternity
By helping others to believe

Broad Shoulders…
Carrying the burdens of others
Strong enough to lean on in stormy weather
Taking on the weight of doing what's right
No grays, only blacks and whites

A Powerful Mind…
Razor-sharp, an entrepreneur of ideas

On the cutting edge of what's new
Willing to go out on a limb
Moving away from what's tried and true

A goal setter, a race finisher
A multi-talented man
Dedicated – honest – fair
Willing to take a stand

A Loving Heart…
So unselfishly generous with his family
A teacher to both old and young
An infinite repertoire of jokes
Lingering on the tip of his tongue

I have your eyes dad
And your quirky sense of humor
I have the love of my son
And you have the love of your daughter

As I look at my precious little Wyatt
Who has those same dancing blue eyes
I ask myself, *Will I be able to teach him by example?*
As you have taught me, by how you live your life

Thank you for teaching me by example Dad
I'll always be proud to call you my father
In all I do and say
I hope people can see I'm your daughter

With Love,
Your Youngest Daughter, Julie

Bible Connection:
Bathsheba's Son Follows His Dad's Lead

King David honored his promise to his wife, Bathsheba, by making their son Solomon king. When the time came near for David to die, he told Solomon to be a strong man and do what the Lord required. He told Solomon to walk in the Lord's ways, and keep His commands, laws, and requirements. When Solomon became king, he showed his love for the Lord by walking according to the statutes of his father David. (I Kings 1:17, 29-30; 2:1-3; 3:3)

Personal Connection
Role #3: Mother

As mothers, there are moments that jealousy can creep into our hearts when we see our children preferring their father to us. We may feel somewhat hurt, wondering why our children seem to think *Dad is so great*, and *Mom is just mom*. However, each time Solomon accomplished something amazing for the Lord, I imagine Bathsheba was happy he'd seen his father as "great" enough to imitate. I imagine this made the Lord happy too. Maybe it's not so bad being *just Mom*, and if our children see their father as a hero for taking out the garbage, the garbage will keep being taken out – which is something to appreciate after all.

 A Welcome Retreat

Prayer to Share (with children): *Lord, I'm so glad that our children love their father, and I love him too.*
Question: Are you jealous when "Dad's the favorite"?
Contemporary Music – *Worship* CD:
  Song Title: *"Above All"* – Track 6
Traditional Music – *Ryman Gospel Reunion* CD:
  Song Title: *"Wait'll You See My Brand New Home"*–Track 19

Chapter 8: Day 4

The Cost of Jealousy and Greed

> The real measure of our wealth is how much
> we should be worth if we lost our money.
> - J.H. Jowett

When I was growing up, going to the "big city of Sioux Falls" was a rare treat. On one of those trips, I found myself staring longingly at a candy cart in a store. I knew my parents wouldn't buy me the candy if I asked them to, so I secretly put a few peppermints in my pocket.

Later, at the end of the drive back home, I began eating my candy. My dad asked what I had in my mouth, and I mumbled, "Candy". Dad instantly pulled the car over and asked me where I'd gotten it. When I told him, I saw his eyes fill with intense anger. He silently turned the car around and drove all the way back to the store so I could apologize and pay the two cents that my candy had cost.

As an adult, I now realize that we did not have much money growing up. This thought never occurred to me as a child, even though we lived in an older farmhouse and had no brand name clothes, no new cars, and no high-tech toys. Maybe that's because my parents didn't define wealth by the amount of material possessions they owned. That's why when I stole the candy, it deeply disappointed my dad and things could only be made right by driving back to the store to pay for the candy.

As parents, we help our children define wealth by the choices we make. If we sacrifice doing what is right for the sake of monetary gain, our children will have a worldly definition of wealth that is based on material things.

BIBLE CONNECTION: A RICH MAN LEARNS THE COST OF GREED

Jesus told this parable: A rich man considered himself wealthy because he lived in luxury every day. A beggar, who believed in God, laid at the rich man's gate, longing to eat his crumbs. When the beggar died, angels carried him to Abraham's side. When the rich man died, he went to hell. He looked up to Abraham, and asked the beggar to come give him water. But Abraham told him, "Son, remember that in your lifetime you received good things, while the beggar received bad things. Now he's comforted here and you're in agony. Between us and you a great chasm has been fixed, and you can't cross over. (Luke 16:19-26)

PERSONAL CONNECTION
ROLE #4: TEACHER

The rich man had a worldly definition of wealth, but the beggar was wealthy because of his faith. Which person would you rather be at the end? As teachers of our children, let's choose not to define our wealth by the amount of material possessions we have. Instead, let's measure our wealth by what we would be worth if we lost our money. Then, our children will learn that faith has eternal value that provides more riches than we can imagine.

 A WELCOME RETREAT

Prayer to Share (with children): *Our wealth comes from our relationship with the Lord rather than the things that we buy.*
Question: How do your children define wealth?
Contemporary Music – ***Worship*** **CD:**
  Song Title: *"Above All"* – Track 6
Traditional Music – ***Ryman Gospel Reunion*** **CD:**
  Song Title: *"Wait'll You See My Brand New Home"* –Track 19

Chapter 8: Day 5

Reflecting on Jealousy, Envy, and Greed

Role #1: Christian Woman
What is your greatest source of jealousy? Why? What needs to change?

Role #2: Wife
How are you controlling your jealousy when it comes to dealing with your husband?

Role #3: Mother
Do you admit to being jealous when "Dad's the favorite"? Think about how to handle that jealousy.

Role #4: Teacher
Teach your children that wealth comes from their relationship with the Lord rather than from the things that they buy.

A Welcome Retreat

Prayer to Share: *As a Christian woman, a wife, a mother, and a teacher, help me to stand strong against jealousy, envy, and greed.*
Contemporary Music: *"Above All"*
  Music Connection: All of the wealth and the wonders of the world cannot compare to the sacrifice Jesus made for you. There is no reason to be jealous, envious, or greedy about earthly things.
Traditional Music: *"Wait'll You See My Brand New Home"*
  Music Connection: When you begin to covet the things of this world, remember that your heavenly Father is building you a brand new home that is more beautiful and rare than anything here on earth.

Worry is spiritual
nearsightedness,
a fumbling way of looking
at little things,
and of magnifying their value.

~ John Benton

Prepare Your Heart

Prayer:
As a Christian woman, a wife, a mother, and a teacher, help me to turn my worries over to You.

Role #1: Christian Woman
Worrying Accomplishes Nothing

Role #2: Wife
Worrying about Relatives

Role #3: Mother
Worrying – Will They Turn Out Right?

Role #4: Teacher
Worrying about Our Children's Faith

Contemporary Music Connection:
"Let It Rain"
Sometimes it seems like worries are pouring down on you all at once. In times like these, remember the Lord's powerful enough to rule over the world. He will see you through any worries you have.

Traditional Music Connection:
"Sheltered in the Arms of Love"
When you begin to worry, close your eyes to recall you are held safely in the grasp of God's love. In that location, not a thing can harm you.

 ## Chapter 9: Day 1

Worrying Accomplishes Nothing

> There are people who are always anticipating trouble, and in this way they manage to enjoy many sorrows that never really happen.
> - Josh Billings

If you take how much you worry and multiply it by 100, that's probably about how much I worry. One of the things I worry the most about is Rich traveling overnight. I worry about him having a car accident, a rapist breaking into our house, someone kidnapping the kids, a tornado destroying our home, and just about anything else imaginable.

One night when Rich was gone, I heard groaning and scraping sounds coming from outside. Without my contacts in, I blindly fumbled with the door and grabbed Wyatt's plastic bat as a weapon. There was a large dog in our front yard, moaning and staggering around. I slammed the door and locked it. In our backyard part of our fence was missing, and there was a hole in the ground beneath it. I locked the doors, took the phone to bed, put the quilt rack in front of my bedroom door, and tossed and turned the rest of the night as I prayed for protection.

In the morning, I put the clues together…our dog, Sage, was in the yard, another dog was injured, and a hole was dug under a missing fence section… AHA! No one was trying to break in to harm the kids and me, a dog had set his sights on Sage. He'd dug a hole under our fence, gotten stuck under it, and pushed it up so hard that he ripped out the whole fence section. The fence then dropped on him, injuring him and leaving him staggering in pain to find his way home. Poor dog, and to think I almost hit him with a bat too. I guess a better plan in the future is for me to try to stop worrying and arm myself with the Lord's armor... rather than poor eyesight, a plastic bat, and a quilt rack.

BIBLE CONNECTION:
A WIDOW OF ZARAPHETH PUSHES WORRY ASIDE

Elijah was worried about finding food and water during a drought when God sent him to a widow in Zarapheth. The widow was worried about the same thing because she only had a handful of flour and a little oil. She was getting ready to make a final meal for herself and her son, but she put her trust in God and shared with Elijah anyway. Elijah told her that God said the jar of flour would not be used up and the jug of oil would not run dry until rain came again, and then there was food every day for all of them. (I Kings 17:9-15)

PERSONAL CONNECTION
ROLE #1: CHRISTIAN WOMAN

Instead of worrying about starving, this widow took a leap of faith and was rewarded with a miracle. As Christian women, let's try to stop worrying and turn our concerns over to the Lord. He might have a miracle in store for us, just waiting for a little bit of faith to set it into motion.

A WELCOME RETREAT

Prayer to Share: *Lord, forgive me for the times I worry. Help me to remember that faith in You is my best response to worrying.*
Question: When you worry, how do you try to combat it?
Contemporary Music – *Worship* CD:
  Song Title: *"Let It Rain"* – Track 8
Traditional Music – *Ryman Gospel Reunion* CD:
  Song Title: *"Sheltered in the Arms of Love"* – Track 8

Chapter 9: Day 2

Worrying about Relatives

> Worry a little bit every day and in a lifetime you will lose a couple of years. If something is wrong, fix it if you can. But train yourself not to worry.
> Worry never fixes anything.
> - Mary Hemingway

Rich and I had similar upbringings, but one thing that was different was the way we vacationed. Rich's family went on multiple fishing trips, and my family went on one big summer vacation. The first time I went fishing with Rich's family, I worried about making a good impression. Things didn't seem to be off to a good start when I saw that Rich's mom wore clothes that covered her from head to toe, and I had on a bathing suit. I felt even more inadequate as I fumbled through casting, catching, reeling, and netting fish.

After about 8 hours of me making these worrisome comparisons, storm clouds rolled in, and the boat began wildly rocking. That's when Rich's mom and I found we had more in common than we knew; we both get motion sickness. She and I huddled together under the hull of the boat, getting sicker and sicker as we made our way back.

She and I still laugh about that day, and I often think God sent that storm just to draw the two of us together. I'll never love fishing quite like Rich does, and he'll never love my family summer vacations quite like I do either. But, our upbringings and families have merged to help Rich and I make the decisions we do. We love our families enough to stop making comparisons and worrying about differences, and in turn, they love us enough to respect our decisions.

Bible Connection:
Michal and David Worry about Relatives

King Saul made comparisons between David and himself, and he worried about the differences he found. Then Saul's daughter Michal fell in love with David. Saul told David he could marry Michal if he killed a hundred enemies. Saul secretly hoped David would be killed, but David wanted to impress Saul so much that he fulfilled the requirement. Saul had no choice but to give Michal to him in marriage. When Saul realized the Lord was with David and that Michal loved him, Saul worried more and more about him. He remained David's enemy the rest of his days. (I Samuel 18:20-29)

Personal Connection
Role #2: Wife

David and Michal had trouble with in-laws from the very start. Since marriage joins two people's families together, there are going to be differences. The decisions we make as a couple will reflect some of each family. As wives, let's try to avoid Saul's mistake of making comparisons and worrying about differences. We are all a part of the family of God, and we need to make lifestyle choices that honor Him, rather than worrying about making choices to please everyone else.

 A Welcome Retreat

Prayer to Share (with husband): *Let's stop worrying about the differences in our families and worry more about pleasing God.*
Question: How often do you worry about relatives?
Contemporary Music – *Worship* CD:
  Song Title: *"Let It Rain"* – Track 8
Traditional Music – *Ryman Gospel Reunion* CD:
  Song Title: *"Sheltered in the Arms of Love"* – Track 8

Chapter 9: Day 3

Worrying — Will They Turn Out Right?

> Every evening, I turn worries over to God.
> He's going to be up all night anyway.
> - Mary C. Crowley

Wyatt was almost two years old, and he was only saying a few words. I worked with him day after day. I read endlessly to him, and I tried to get him to repeat words after me, but nothing seemed to help. Something was wrong.

When I got Wyatt's hearing tested, the results showed a hearing problem in both ears. Fluid was found, and it appeared to have been there for a while. Wyatt had a steroid shot and allergy medication to clear up the fluid. Speech therapy was also suggested, so we made plans for a speech teacher to work with Wyatt 3 times a week at our home. As the time neared for Wyatt's first speech session, I began to worry that the teacher would expect my little 2 year old to sit in a chair and repeat words back to her.

I was having this worry on Wyatt's first day of speech when a bright yellow VW bug zipped into our driveway. A spry little woman jumped out and began carrying bags of toys to the door. She enthusiastically shook my hand and told me to call her Sue. She was bubbly, full of life, and entirely different than what I had expected. Over the next year, I watched as God helped Sue work a miracle with Wyatt. Slowly but surely, Sue helped Wyatt learn to talk.

Now that Wyatt is 5 years old, he talks nonstop. We don't get to see Sue very often anymore, but I will always envision her with a special light around her... a glow that can only come from a spirit-filled woman…an angel sent from the Lord to give our little Wyatt a voice.

BIBLE CONNECTION:
HANNAH COULD HAVE LET WORRY TAKE ROOT

Hannah was worried because she had no children, and she made a vow that if the Lord gave her a son, she would give him to the Lord all the days of his life. The Lord heard her prayer and gave her a son. She praised God and named her son Samuel. By the time he was weaned, she brought him to live at the temple. Each year, Hannah sewed Samuel a new robe and took it to him when she went to the temple for their annual sacrifice. Hannah was content because Samuel grew up in the Lord's presence, and he increased in stature with God and men. (I Samuel 1:11, 19, 24; 2:19, 26)

PERSONAL CONNECTION
ROLE #3: MOTHER

Hannah must have worried about Samuel, just as we worry about our children. Still, Scripture only mentions her praising God. As mothers, let's be like Hannah and turn our worries about our children over to God. This act shows a stronger faith in Him, rather than in ourselves.

 A WELCOME RETREAT

Prayer to Share (with children): *Lord, when I worry about my children, I will depend on Your strength and not my own.*
Question: When you worry about your children, do you turn those worries over to God?
Contemporary Music – *Worship* CD:
  Song Title: *"Let It Rain"* – Track 8
Traditional Music – *Ryman Gospel Reunion* CD:
  Song Title: *"Sheltered in the Arms of Love"* – Track 8

Chapter 9: Day 4

Worrying about Our Children's Faith

> We worry about what a child will be tomorrow,
> yet we forget that he is someone today.
> - Stacia Tauscher

I attended a Mother's Day banquet at our church with my mom, and the table favors were tiny cactus plants grown in miniature ketchup cups. I took mine home, and when it came time for me to go to college, I took the cactus with me. I figured it would be the only plant that would fit in my dorm room, and I knew it would remind me of Mom.

The only problem was that I never unpacked it. For my first two years of college, it stayed in a box and never saw the light of day or received a drop of water. It wasn't until I transferred colleges and moved in with my sister Carrie that I rediscovered the cactus. Amazingly, despite my neglect, the cactus was alive and had even grown several inches.

There is only one other plant that has somehow managed not only to survive, but also to thrive, in my possession. It is the welcome plant I received when I first visited my sister's church after I moved in with her. It was given to me in a church coffee mug, and today it is well over 3 feet tall.

Isn't it ironic that the only two plants I've been able to keep alive are the ones that began their lives at church? By beginning our children's lives at church, we can give them a better chance of surviving too. Spiritual growth can't be forced, but when children are nourished with living water and the light of Christ, growth is in the Master's hands – and there's no hands more capable than His.

Bible Connection:
Sowing the Seed of the Word of God

Jesus told this parable: A farmer went out to sow his seed. As he was scattering the seeds, some fell along the path. They were trampled on and eaten by the birds. Some fell on rocks, and when they came up, the plants withered because they had no moisture. Other seeds fell among the thorns, and the thorns grew and choked the plants. Still other seeds fell on good soil. They came up and yielded a crop, a hundred times more than was sown. (Luke 8:4-8)

Personal Connection
Role #4: Teacher

The farmer didn't stop sowing seeds even though some seemed to have a poor chance of survival. He depended on the Master to provide what was needed for growth to occur. As teachers of our children, it is our responsibility to continue sowing the seed. It is our children's responsibility to hear the Word and respond to it. We can't rush this or force it to happen, but we can persevere and sow the seed, choosing to be confident that our Master will provide the light and the living water that will help our children grow.

 A Welcome Retreat

Prayer to Share (with children): *Lord, when I worry about my children, I will sow Your seed again and depend on You.*
Question: When you worry about your children, do you sow the seed again, and let the Master do His work?
Contemporary Music – *Worship* CD:
  Song Title: *"Let It Rain"* – Track 8
Traditional Music – *Ryman Gospel Reunion* CD:
  Song Title: *"Sheltered in the Arms of Love"* – Track 8

Chapter 9: Day 5

Reflecting on Worry

Role #1: Christian Woman
When was the last time you gave a specific worry over to the Lord? How did it feel after you gave it away?

Role #2: Wife
What circumstances make you worry the most in regard to your relatives? Discuss it with your husband. As a couple, choose a God-honoring response to that circumstance.

Role #3: Mother
Have you been depending on yourself when you are worried about your children? Begin depending on the Lord instead.

Role #4: Teacher
What is your greatest worry about your children right now? Find a similar situation in the Bible, and use the Word as a starting place to talk with your children about your worry.

 A Welcome Retreat

Prayer to Share: *As a Christian woman, a wife, a mother, and a teacher, help me to turn my worries over to You.*

Contemporary Music: *"Let It Rain"*
  Music Connection: Sometimes it seems like worries are pouring down on you all at once. In times like these, remember the Lord's powerful enough to rule over the world. He will see you through any worries you have.

Traditional Music: *"Sheltered in the Arms of Love"*
  Music Connection: When you begin to worry, close your eyes to recall you are held safely in the arms of God's love. In that location, not a thing can harm you.

God takes hold
when we break down.
We go as far as we can
and then God takes hold
when we can't go any farther.

~ A.P. Gouthey

Prepare Your Heart

Prayer:
As a Christian woman, a wife, a mother, and a teacher, help me to turn to You when I am sad.

Role #1: Christian Woman
Sadness and Regrets about Past Sins

Role #2: Wife
Not a Fairy Tale Marriage

Role #3: Mother
The Comfort of a Mother's Arms

Role #4: Teacher
Caring for One Another

Contemporary Music Connection:
"Draw Me Close"
When you are burdened with sadness,
lay it all down before the Lord. He will draw you close
and help you through the saddest of times.

Traditional Music Connection:
"If We Never Meet Again"
As you endure sad times, remember God has
happier times planned for you. Look toward heaven
and know you'll never have sorrow there.

Chapter 10: Day 1

Sadness and Regrets about Past Sins

> When life knocks you to your knees, and it will, get up!
> If it knocks you to your knees again,
> isn't that the best position in which to pray?
> - Ethel Barrymore

I'm an emotional girl, and I've cried my fair share of tears. I'm a quick crier, and the tears usually stop flowing within a few moments, but there have been a few times in my life that I've actually sobbed or wept. Usually those times are associated with deeply painful moments in my life. However, there's one thing that can make me sob at any given time. Do you want to know what it is? It's thinking about those sinful things I've done in the past. I mean the *really* sinful things that I like to forget about ever having done. Those things are so deeply painful, and I think it's because there is so much regret that goes along with them.

My greatest sins took place during the period of my life that I was farthest apart from Christ. I can't tell you how many times I've wished I could turn back time and undo the things I did back then. I wish I could talk to that girl I used to be. I'd help that lost little teenager find Jesus and fill her life up with Him instead of drinking, parties, and boys. I'd help her see that all she needed to be happy was Him, and I'd help her friends see that too.

When I think about my past, it's hard to believe Christ can love me. I know He knows all about my sins, still He doesn't seem to remember them. I don't deserve that grace, but He keeps on loving me anyway. When I think of that kind of mercy, it makes me sob, and I'm in awe of His love.

BIBLE CONNECTION:
A Sinful Woman Who Wept at Jesus' Feet

A woman who had lived a sinful life came to see Jesus as He dined at a Pharisee's house. As she stood beside Jesus, she started weeping so much that she began to wet His feet with her tears. Using her hair to wipe away the tears, she kissed Jesus' feet and poured perfume on them. The Pharisee thought it was wrong for Jesus to allow this sinful woman to do this. But Jesus told the Pharisee that the woman's many sins had been forgiven – for she loved Him so much. Jesus told the woman her faith had saved her, and therefore she could go in peace. (Luke 7:36-39; 47-50)

Personal Connection
Role #1: Christian Woman

The deep, deep regret and shame of sin can make us feel like we are not worthy of God's grace. As Christian women, when that little voice inside us says *maybe I'm not good enough for God*, let's think of what Jesus had to say to this sinful woman. Then let's hold fast to the peace that goes along with receiving God's mercy, and let's keep on loving Him, just as He keeps on loving us.

A Welcome Retreat

Prayer to Share: *Lord, I'm so sad about my sins, and I pray for Your forgiveness. Let the peace of Your mercy wash over me and make me whole again.*

Question: Does the sadness you feel about your sins prevent you from feeling completely loved by God?

Contemporary Music – *Worship* CD:
  Song Title: *"Draw Me Close"* – Track 3

Traditional Music – *Ryman Gospel Reunion* CD:
  Song Title: *"If We Never Meet Again"* – Track 20

Chapter 10: Day 2

Not a Fairy Tale Marriage

> It is only possible to live happily-ever-after
> on a day-to-day basis.
> - Margaret Bonano

My Grandpa and Grandma Star got married when they were teenagers. They worked hard to provide a good life for their family, and there was plenty of love to go around. My Grandma Star was about 40 years old when she began to notice a change in her sight. She had difficulty seeing things peripherally, and it wasn't long until she had tunnel vision. Objects became more and more out of focus, until all she could see were light and dark shapes. Eventually, even that faded into a solid white picture, and my Grandma had become totally blind by the time she was 55 years old.

Grandpa and she made the best of it. She cooked and cleaned, and Grandpa helped her learn how to get around. Grandma *never* complained about being blind. In fact, she never even mentioned it. Grandpa didn't either, and they seemed content to go through life together, hand-in-hand.

About six months ago, Grandma began to get lost in their house. Grandpa would find her in the garage or on her hands and knees in the living room, and he would lead her back to her chair. Then, Grandpa fell off a ladder. Migraine headaches made it too difficult for him to care for Grandma, so they moved into an assisted living home. After that, Grandpa could have been off somewhere doing more entertaining things, but his favorite place to be was still beside the woman he calls "wife", holding her hand, and loving her no matter what, until the very end.

BIBLE CONNECTION:
THE SADNESS OF THE PARENTS OF A BLIND SON

A man that had been blind since birth was begging along the road. When the disciples saw him, they asked Jesus whether the man or his parents had sinned, since it was a common belief that suffering was the result of a great sin. Jesus said neither the man nor his parents had sinned. Instead, the man was blind so that the work of God could be displayed in his life. Jesus then spit on the ground and made some mud with the saliva. He put the mud on the man's eyes and told him to wash in the pool of Siloam. So the man did, and he came home seeing. (John 9:1-7)

PERSONAL CONNECTION
ROLE #2: WIFE

Blindness could have destroyed this man's life and his parents' lives because it was considered to be the result of their sins. Blindness could have tainted my grandparents' marriage too, because it made many simple things difficult. However, my grandparents chose happiness over sadness. As wives, we can live happily-ever-after with our husbands on a daily basis. This kind of bite-sized love is more real than a fairy tale, and it has the longevity of a lifetime.

A WELCOME RETREAT

Prayer to Share (with husband): *Lord, help my husband and I to overcome sadness hand-in-hand, with You by our side.*
Question: How do you and your husband cope with sadness?
Contemporary Music – *Worship* CD:
  Song Title: *"Draw Me Close"* – Track 3
Traditional Music – *Ryman Gospel Reunion* CD:
  Song Title: *"If We Never Meet Again"* – Track 20

Chapter 10: Day 3

The Comfort of a Mother's Arms

> A mother's arms are more comforting than anyone else's.
> - Diana, Princess of Wales

One of the saddest times I can remember is when my family moved from our farm to town. Leaving the only home I'd ever known was only the tip of the pain I felt. My sister Cindy had just gotten married, and she and her husband were going to continue living far away from us. My sister Carrie, who had been a big part of my life, was leaving to attend college for four years. My mother had gone back to work as a teacher, and my dad was pursuing a new career. I felt like my family was being pulled in all different directions, and I didn't know where I fit anymore.

I was a teenager, and I cried…and cried…and cried. I used an entire roll of toilet paper to dry my tears during the first week in our new home. I remember my mother holding me in her arms and crying too. Every time my mother wrapped her arms around me, I felt a little more secure and a little more sure I'd be alright.

There were some tough times at first, but everyone tried to make me feel better about the situation. Carrie came home to watch me play sports, cheer, and sing. Cindy made the long trip home every holiday, and she came to as many of my activities as she could. My parents never missed attending one of my activities, and they did their best to surround me with love. Little by little, the pain began to ease. I didn't feel like I'd lost my sisters anymore, although I still missed them deeply, and life became livable again.

Bible Connection: Rizpah Mourns the Loss of Her Sons

Rizpah mourned the loss of her two sons, who were killed because of their father's sins. Rizpah took sackcloth and spread it out for herself on a rock. From the beginning to the end of harvest, Rizpah guarded her sons' bodies. She did not let the birds of the day or the wild animals of the night touch them. When King David heard what Rizpah was doing, he took the bones of her husband and her sons and gave them a proper buriel. (II Samuel 21:8-14)

Personal Connection
Role #3: Mother

Rizpah's pain at the loss of her sons caused her to guard their bodies from being desecrated from April to October. That's a long time, but a mother's love doesn't know the boundaries of time. A mother's love is eternal, and it lasts through the most difficult periods of life. My mother loved me through the toughest times in my life, and it's one of the many reasons I love her so much today. As mothers, let's love our children through the sad times in their lives. Even though we may not understand it, let's wrap our arms around them and stay by their side until the pain has eased.

 A Welcome Retreat

Prayer to Share (with children): *Lord, when my children are sad help them to find comfort in my arms until their pain has eased.*
Question: How do you respond to your children when they are sad?
Contemporary Music – *Worship* CD:
  Song Title: *"Draw Me Close"* – Track 3
Traditional Music – *Ryman Gospel Reunion* CD:
  Song Title: *"If We Never Meet Again"* – Track 20

Chapter 10: Day 4

Caring for One Another

> Even if you can't prevent another's sorrow, caring will lessen it.
> - Frank A. Clark

When we were growing up, a girl named Collette attended church with us. She had special needs that caused her to seizure. She needed help walking, and she drooled as she spoke with a pronounced slur. Her mental capacity was that of a small child, but she was in her upper teens. Because of this, she was placed in my sister Carrie's junior high Sunday school class.

Collette's eyes practically lit up whenever she saw Carrie because every Sunday, Carrie took Collette to Sunday school. After Sunday school, Carrie helped Collette walk up several flights of steps. Then, Carrie took her to the library to help her check out books, and the next Sunday the routine started all over again. Carrie's classmates also tried to be accepting of Collette, but no one chose to love her like Carrie did. Collette couldn't use eloquent words to express her gratitude, but she often clumsily touched Carrie's face and said in a childlike voice, "Love you."

I see Carrie teaching her children to have the same kind of love. At our church, an elderly man named Chris looks at Carrie and her children with the same light in his eyes that I remember Collette having. Just like Collette, he finds joy in knowing Carrie and her children will talk to him, hold his hand, and spend a little time with him each Sunday. Most people walk right by him, but Carrie and her children stop, visit a while, and make an old man feel loved once again.

BIBLE CONNECTION: THE GOOD SAMARITAN CARES FOR A STRANGER

Jesus told this parable: A man who was traveling was robbed, stripped, beaten, and left half dead along the road. A priest came down the road, but when he saw the man, he passed by on the other side. A Levite came down the road, but he also chose to pass by. A Samaritan came down the road, and when he saw the man, he bandaged his wounds, put him on his donkey, and took him to an inn to care for him. The next day, he paid the innkeeper two silver coins to look after the man, promising to reimburse him for extra expenses when he returned. Of the three men, only the Samaritan was a good neighbor because he showed mercy. (Luke 10:30-37)

PERSONAL CONNECTION
ROLE #4: TEACHER

The Samaritan didn't have to stop and help this stranger, but he chose to have mercy on him out of love. My sister Carrie is a modern day Samaritan because she chooses to love people who desperately need to be loved. As teachers of our children, let's teach our children to be merciful and to love the unlovable by being good Samaritans ourselves.

 A WELCOME RETREAT

Prayer to Share (with children): *Lord, help my children to show mercy and love to people, especially those desperately needing it.*
Question: Do you have a merciful and loving attitude toward people who are less easy to love?
Contemporary Music – *Worship* CD:
  Song Title: *"Draw Me Close"* – Track 3
Traditional Music – *Ryman Gospel Reunion* CD:
  Song Title: *"If We Never Meet Again"* – Track 20

Chapter 10: Day 5

Reflecting on Sadness

Role #1: Christian Woman
What sins do you regret the most? Pray about each of those sins, and ask for forgiveness. Then, believe Christ's death was sacrifice enough to wipe those sins clean. Accept His mercy and allow yourself to be at peace with your past.

Role #2: Wife
Are you sad that you don't have a fairy tale marriage? Begin to live happily-ever-after by choosing to find things to love about your husband one day at a time.

Role #3: Mother
When your children are sad, wrap your arms around them in a comforting hug, and let them be the first to stop hugging.

Role #4: Teacher
Teach your children to care about others. Even if they don't understand the person's sadness, caring will lessen it.

 A Welcome Retreat

Prayer to Share: *As a Christian woman, a wife, a mother, and a teacher, help me to turn to You when I am sad.*

Contemporary Music: *"Draw Me Close"*
  Music Connection: When you are burdened with sadness, lay it all down before the Lord. He will draw you close and help you through the saddest of times.

Traditional Music: *"If We Never Meet Again"*
  Music Connection: As you endure sad times, remember God has happier times planned for you. Look toward heaven and know you'll never have sorrow there.

No matter how big and tough a problem may be, get rid of confusion by taking one little step towards solution. Do something. Then try again. At the worst, so long as you don't do it the same way twice, you will eventually use up all the wrong ways of doing it and thus the next try will be the right one.

- George F. Nordenholt

Prepare Your Heart

Prayer:
As a Christian woman, a wife, a mother, and a teacher, help me to seek Your guidance when I'm confused.

Role #1: Christian Woman
Confused about How to Solve a Problem

Role #2: Wife
Confusion Caused by Poor Communication

Role #3: Mother
When Your Children Are Confused

Role #4: Teacher
Confused about What's Right and Wrong

Contemporary Music Connection:
"Draw Me Close"
When you're feeling confused, ask the Lord for His guidance. He will draw you close to Him and make it clear what you should do.

Traditional Music Connection:
"Dig a Little Deeper in God's Love"
Your life will have trials you don't understand. In those confusing times, dig deep in the reservoir of God's love, and He'll guide you through the confusion.

Chapter 11: Day 1

Confused about How to Solve a Problem

> The basic problem most people have is that they're doing nothing to solve their basic problem.
> - Bob Richardson

I'd owned my copy/print/fax/scan/"do anything" machine for several years, when a piece of paper got jammed in it. I yanked it out, and after that, every time I tried to use the machine, the paper got jammed. I called the store where I'd purchased it, and they said I'd have to ship it to a repair shop across the United States, pay $150 for it even to be looked at, pay parts and labor, and pay to have it shipped back. That did NOT sound like the best plan to me, so they gave me a 1-800 phone number to call instead.

When I called, they said the charge would be $35 per minute, since my warranty had expired. *At that rate*, I politely told them, *I'd probably be able to purchase a dozen new "do anything" machines.* They quickly gave me a website with troubleshooting tips on it, and they stressed that it would be FREE. I did not have much faith in "virtual help", since from past experience I knew it meant that there was *virtually* no person to *help* you, and I began wondering if my "do anything" machine would ever "do anything" again.

That's when I prayed about it and asked God to help me fix the problem. I felt led to give the website a chance, but my faith wavered when the directions said to fold a piece of paper and jam it under the paper tray. It was tough to believe a paper-jamming problem could be solved by jamming in a paper, but I was desperate, so I tried it anyway. It actually worked – in fact, it's been working for 2 years. It just goes to prove that God can handle ANY problem, even a technical one, if we just remember to ask.

Bible Connection:
A Young Maid Solves Naaman's Problem

Naaman had leprosy, and his wife's young maid said the Lord's prophet in Samaria would cure him. So, Naaman took many expensive gifts, and went with his horses and chariots to the prophet Elisha's house. Elisha did not even come out to see Naaman. Instead, he sent his messenger to say, "Go, wash yourself seven times in the Jordan, and your flesh will be restored, and you will be cleansed." Naaman was angry about this at first, but he finally dipped himself in the Jordon seven times. His flesh was restored and became clean like that of a young boy. (II Kings 5:2-5, 9-14)

Personal Connection
Role #1: Christian Woman

Naaman was a wealthy man, and he thought Elisha would cure his leprosy if he brought him expensive gifts. But, Elisha wanted Naaman to know God was the One who cured him. As Christian women, we have to quit relying on our own resources to solve our problems. God can handle any problem, so save some time by calling on Him first.

A Welcome Retreat

Prayer to Share: *Lord, help me look to You to solve my problems.*
Question: When you have a problem, do you rely on your own resources, instead of asking God for help first?
Contemporary Music – *Worship* CD:
  Song Title: *"Draw Me Close"* – Track 3
Traditional Music – *Ryman Gospel Reunion* CD:
  Song Title: *"Dig a Little Deeper in God's Love"* – Track 17

Chapter 11: Day 2
Confusion Caused by Poor Communication

> Half the world's problems are caused by poor communications. The other half are caused by good communications.
> - Anonymous

Rich and I were planning to take a trip to California for our honeymoon the summer after we got married, but it was five years later when we were finally able to go. I was so excited! I knew I'd finally have the romantic honeymoon I'd always imagined. I envisioned intimate conversations, long walks together on the beach, and hotel room service.

Rich insisted on making the vacation plans, and I thought that was so romantic. As the time for our departure neared, I asked Rich for a description of our hotel accommodations. That's when he told me we'd be staying with his aunt, in her basement. I began to realize that Rich had a very different idea of how this vacation was going to go.

When we arrived in California, Rich's aunt picked us up, and we spent the day together. The next morning, we rented a little truck to cart around Rich's surfboard. We went to the beach, and Rich became a little dot on a surfboard that waved to me every half an hour or so.

After several days of this, I shed a few tears as I told Rich how I'd imagined the trip going. After our talk, we dressed up and went to the Beachhouse Restaurant. We stayed there for hours, eating seafood, watching the sun go down over the ocean, and listening to romantic music. It was so beautiful, and it was a perfect romantic ending to our trip.

BIBLE CONNECTION:
CONFUSION DURING ABRAM AND SARAI'S TRIP

Abram and Sarai traveled to Egypt to live there during a famine. Sarai was very beautiful, and Abram feared that the Egyptians would kill him and take her for themselves. He told Sarai to say she was his sister, so they'd both be safe. When the Egyptians saw her, they praised her and took her to Pharaoh. He treated Abram well for her sake, and gave him many gifts. The Lord inflicted diseases on Pharaoh and his household, and then He revealed Sarai's true identity to Pharaoh. Pharaoh asked Abram why he hadn't said Sarai was his wife. Then he told them to go. (Genesis 12:10-20)

PERSONAL CONNECTION
ROLE #2: WIFE

Sarai's trip to Egypt probably didn't go quite like she'd expected it to. She wasn't Abram's full sister, but she was his half-sister, so she most certainly didn't envision this slight miscommunication having the effect it did. Blessedly, the Lord stepped in and revealed Sarai's true identity. As wives, let's keep communication open with our husbands. Things still may not go the way we envisioned, but at least our husbands won't be confused about the situation.

 A WELCOME RETREAT

Prayer to Share (with husband): *Lord, help me communicate openly with my husband, so my response is not confusing to him.*
Question: When things don't go the way you envisioned, do you first consider how openly you communicated?
Contemporary Music – *Worship* CD:
  Song Title: *"Draw Me Close"* – Track 3
Traditional Music – *Ryman Gospel Reunion* CD:
  Song Title: *"Dig a Little Deeper in God's Love"* – Track 17

Chapter 11: Day 3

When Your Children Are Confused

> The measure of success is not whether you have a tough problem to deal with, but whether it's the same problem you had last year.
> - John Foster Dulles

My brother-in-law, Dave, was going to come visit us while he was in town on business. When I told Wyatt that Dave was coming to visit, he was very excited, and he began asking question after question about him. He asked what Dave would do while he was here, and he asked if he would be able to see him and talk to him. I was kind of confused about his questions, but he was 4 years old, and he hadn't seen Dave for a while, so I figured he didn't remember him.

Over the next few days, the questions got stranger and stranger. Wyatt kept saying, "Dave's just a little guy, right mom?" Dave isn't very tall, so I agreed, but I said that Dave was a tough guy who had no trouble hiking up mountains or running for miles on a treadmill. Then, Wyatt kept saying, "Dave's a tough, brave little guy, right mom?"

I was so relieved when Dave finally came to visit. As we ate supper together, Wyatt kept staring at Dave, and he seemed to be in awe of him. Later, Wyatt raced out to wave goodbye and ask him to come back soon. As Dave drove away, Wyatt asked me if Dave could show him how to use a sling next time. All of the odd questions finally made sense; Wyatt thought Dave was "David" from the Bible. Wyatt is 5 ½ now, and he still thinks his Uncle Dave is a pretty great guy. However, he does know Dave won't be teaching him how to pick 5 smooth stones and use a sling anytime soon.

Bible Connection:
Belshazzar's Mother Seeks Daniel's Help

King Belshazzar gave a banquet, and he and his guests drank wine from the goblets taken from the temple of God. Suddenly the fingers of a human hand appeared and wrote on the wall. Belshazzar was so frightened and confused that his knees knocked together, and his legs gave way. His mother told him to call Daniel to interpret the writing. She said Daniel was a man of God that had insight, intelligence, and wisdom. Daniel told Belshazzar the writing meant God had numbered the days of his reign and brought them to an end. That very night the king was slain. (Daniel 5:1-30)

Personal Connection
Role #3: Mother

Belshazzar's mother knew Daniel would be able to use God's help to make sense out of all the confusion, but by then it was too late for Belshazzar. As mothers, we can expect our children to be confused and in need of direction. Let's not be like Belshazzar's mother and wait until it's too late. Let's seek God's help as soon as the problem arises. Problems do not go away on their own, so seek God right away, before they become a way of life.

 A Welcome Retreat

Prayer to Share (with children): *Lord, when my children are confused and have a problem, we will seek Your guidance together.*
Question: When your children are confused or have a problem to solve, do you seek God's guidance?
Contemporary Music – *Worship* CD:
  Song Title: *"Draw Me Close"* – Track 3
Traditional Music – *Ryman Gospel Reunion* CD:
  Song Title: *"Dig a Little Deeper in God's Love"* – Track 17

Chapter 11: Day 4

Confused about What's Right and Wrong

> Right is right even if everyone is against it.
> Wrong is wrong even if everyone is for it.
> - William Penn

We'd lost almost every volleyball game in the season, and it looked like this game was going to end in the same way. It was game point, and we were extremely behind when it was my teammate's turn to serve. She threw the ball in the air, arced back her arm, and smacked it with an impressive hit. Unfortunately, it did not clear the net. The other team easily scored the winning point, and we'd lost…again.

We politely shook hands with the other team, but back in the locker room, things were not nearly so cordial. A group of girls backed the girl who had netted the last serve into a corner. She was crying as they began taunting her by saying she had lost the game. The words *This is wrong!* kept going through my mind and without really thinking I shouted, "Leave her alone! I mean, we all played terrible out there. You can't really believe it was just her fault that we lost?"

I was usually a quiet girl, and I think they were all shocked because they backed off. The locker room cleared, and soon it was just the girl who'd missed the serve and me. I was surprised when she said, "Don't ever do that again. Now I won't be popular. Those girls will never be my friends again." I shook my head and said, "But they never were." Things were strained between us after that, but I persisted in being polite. Years later, she told me I was right that day in the locker room because those girls were not her friends. Then, she thanked me for always being nice to her.

BIBLE CONNECTION: A FRIEND PERSISTS TO DO THE RIGHT THING

Jesus told this parable: Suppose a man has a friend, and he goes to him at midnight and says, "Lend me three loaves of bread, because a friend of mine has come to me on a journey, and I have nothing to set before him." But the one inside does not want to be bothered and refuses to get up and open the door to give him anything. I tell you, though he will not get up and give him the bread, because of the man's bold persistence, he will finally get up and give him as much as he needs. (Luke 11:5-8)

PERSONAL CONNECTION
ROLE #4: TEACHER

If you've ever been standing at the crossroads of right and wrong, you know how hard it can be to persist through obstacles to do the right thing. Then, even after you do the right thing, the right outcome may not follow. As teachers of our children, we need to teach them that *right is still right if everyone is against it, and wrong is still wrong if everyone is for it.* We need to persist in being sure our children clearly know what's right and what's wrong, so there's no confusion about what behavior is imitative of Jesus.

 A WELCOME RETREAT

Prayer to Share (with children): *I want to teach my children to know what is right and wrong, so they can be more like Jesus.*
Question: When your children are confused if something is right or wrong, do you give them clear answers?
Contemporary Music – *Worship* CD:
  Song Title: *"Draw Me Close"* – Track 3
Traditional Music – *Ryman Gospel Reunion* CD:
  Song Title: *"Dig a Little Deeper in God's Love"* – Track 17

Chapter 11: Day 5

Reflecting on Confusion

Role #1: Christian Woman
Are you feeling confused about how to solve a problem? Don't rely on your own resources; ask God for help today.

Role #2: Wife
How can you better communicate to your husband what you are thinking? Remember, men appreciate fewer well-chosen words rather than many words as you think aloud.

Role #3: Mother
How have you responded to your children when they're confused? Make seeking God a part of your response.

Role #4: Teacher
Do your children know what is right and wrong in God's eyes? Be ready to give clear direction to them when sticky situations arise.

 A Welcome Retreat

Prayer to Share: *As a Christian woman, a wife, a mother, and a teacher, help me to seek Your guidance when I'm confused.*
Contemporary Music: *"Draw Me Close"*
  Music Connection: When you're feeling confused, ask the Lord for His guidance. He will draw you close to Him and make it clear what you should do.
Traditional Music: *"Dig a Little Deeper in God's Love"*
  Music Connection: Your life will have trials you don't understand. In those confusing times, dig deep in the reservoir of God's love, and He'll guide you through the confusion.

Prepare Your Heart

Prayer:
Help my thoughts as a Christian woman, a wife, a mother, and a teacher to reflect Your influence in my life.

Role #1: Christian Woman
Thoughtful Thoughts

Role #2: Wife
Thoughts Often Become Words

Role #3: Mother
Thoughts about Being a Mother

Role #4: Teacher
Self-Absorbed Thoughts

Contemporary Music Connection:
"Breathe"
No one can hear all of your thoughts but the Lord.
When you worship Him with all of your mind,
it shows His presence is alive in you.

Traditional Music Connection:
"Turn Your Radio On"
Control your thoughts
by staying in touch with God
and listening for His call.

Chapter 12: Day 1

Thoughtful Thoughts

> Our minds can shape the way a thing will be because we act according to our expectations.
> - Federico Fellini

My co-worker's first precious granddaughter was going to be born that afternoon, and he excitedly told all of us, "Today is the day I've been waiting for. Today I become a grandpa!"

He eagerly anticipated the baby's arrival, but when she was born, she was diagnosed with Down's Syndrome. He was devastated, and a cloud seemed to hang over him throughout the day. A hush came over the building, and no one quite knew what to say to him.

Later that day, I walked into his office and asked him how he was doing. He said, "All day, I've had person after person come in to offer their condolences and tell me how sorry they are to hear about my granddaughter. But then, Diane came in. She threw her arms around me and spun me around shouting, *"Congratulations old man! You're finally a grandpa!"* She blew a party horn, and had some funny 'over the hill grandpa' gifts for me. I guess I will never forget her for that, and I will always be so thankful."

As I gave him a hug, I thought of how close I'd just been to being one more person to offer him my condolences. We all thought it was so sad that his granddaughter had Down's Syndrome, but Diane thought how wonderful it was for her to be born. Her thoughts were more thoughtful, and he appreciated her reaction so much more.

Bible Connection: A Woman Discovers Jesus Is Thoughtful

Jesus asked a Samaritan woman to draw water for Him at the well. She thought she couldn't, since Samaritans did not associate with Jews. Jesus knew her thoughts and told her God's gift of *living water* is available to all who ask for it. She was surprised at Jesus' thoughtfulness and wanted to know more. Jesus told her to get her husband and come back, but she said she had no husband. Jesus revealed He already knew she'd had five husbands and was living with a man that wasn't her husband. She left her water jar and told everyone that she had met the Christ because He was able to tell her all that she had ever done. (John 4:7-19, 28-29)

Personal Connection
Role #1: Christian Woman

The Samaritan woman probably went to the well alone because she felt everyone thought poorly of her. However, Jesus only thought of offering her "living water". As Christian women, let's try to keep our thoughts thoughtful. Let's also keep our thoughts going in the right direction, since they often influence the way a thing will go.

   A Welcome Retreat

Prayer to Share: *I want my thoughts to be pleasing to You, Lord. Help me to be thoughtful in my thoughts, just as Jesus was with the Samaritan woman.*

Question: Do you remember to keep your thoughts thoughtful, so you can worship God with your mind?

Contemporary Music – *Worship* CD:
  Song Title: *"Breathe"* – Track 7

Traditional Music – *Ryman Gospel Reunion* CD:
  Song Title: *"Turn Your Radio On"* – Track 1

Chapter 12: Day 2

Thoughts Often Become Words

> Be careful of your thoughts;
> they may become words at any moment.
> - Ira Gassen

What do you think about your husband? I've always thought of my husband Rich as being an incredibly strong man, who is very in control in even the most out-of-control situations. He has such a sense of security and self-assurance about him, and I depend on that quality in difficult times.

One of these difficult times was when we went to the hospital to have our first baby. As I began having hard labor, he began turning as white as a ghost. He woozily shimmied to the bathroom, and unsteadily shut the door. I could hear the water running…and running…and running… and I began to realize that my in-control husband was not so in-control as the minutes ticked by.

Because our baby was going to be so premature, there were no less than 10 people in the delivery room. After 15 minutes of Rich's holing up in the bathroom, not a single person was by my side. They were all crowded around the bathroom door to check on Rich. During a particularly hard contraction, I shouted for Rich to "get out of that bathroom and come help me with this baby". He returned unsteadily on his feet, and I've always been glad that I held my tongue at that point and said no more.

Apparently, Rich was not so self-assured when it came to me having a baby. I still think of Rich as being a self-assured man, but I have a deeper understanding of things that do shake him up. He's not less of a man because of this reaction, he's more of a man, because he cares.

BIBLE CONNECTION: MICHAL'S THOUGHTS BECOME WORDS

Michal saw her husband, King David, leaping and dancing for joy in the street as the ark was brought home, and she despised him in her heart. Michal came out to meet David and said mockingly, "How the king distinguished himself today, disrobing in the sight of the slave girls of his servants as any common fellow would!" David said he was celebrating before the Lord, and he'd continue do so, even if he did appear undignified. After this dispute, Michal had no children to the day of her death. (II Samuel 6:14-23)

PERSONAL CONNECTION ROLE #2: WIFE

Michal thought David's behavior as a king should be very dignified, and when she saw him dancing in the street, she said some spiteful words. As wives, we need to think good thoughts about our husbands. Then, when our thoughts become words, we will only have reason to be glad.

 A WELCOME RETREAT

Prayer to Share (with husband): *Lord, help me to think good thoughts about my husband because they affect what I say.*
Question: Are the thoughts you replay in your mind about your husband mostly good or bad?
Contemporary Music – *Worship* CD:
  Song Title: *"Breathe"* – Track 7
Traditional Music – *Ryman Gospel Reunion* CD:
  Song Title: *"Turn Your Radio On"* – Track 1

Chapter 12: Day 3

Thoughts about Being a Mother

> Remember the wonderful blessings that come to you each day from the hands of a generous God, and forget the irritations that would detract from your happiness.
> - William Arthur Ward

I wanted to be a mother more than anything in the world, but my first pregnancy had ended in a miscarriage. I was cautiously excited about my second pregnancy, however, it wasn't long before I was having preterm labor. Bedrest was successful for a while, but at 32 ½ weeks, my water broke.

We rushed to the hospital, trying not to panic. A doctor immediately did an ultrasound and found more bad news; our baby had a hole in his heart. I was already having hard labor, and less than 2 hours later, our baby Wyatt was born. We barely got to see him before he was whisked away.

We spent the next 2 ½ weeks in intensive care. Wyatt looked so tiny beneath all of the tubes and monitors. He struggled his way through breathing, feeding, jaundice, and apnea. However, the hole in his heart couldn't be found. The cardiologists were baffled, but they eventually concurred that Wyatt had a perfectly healthy heart.

It seemed significant that we got to take Wyatt home on Christmas Eve. As I gazed upon my miracle baby Wyatt, I felt a bit of the awe that Mary must have felt when she gazed upon her miracle baby Jesus. When I rocked him to sleep, I thanked God for our son, and I vowed to remember how blessed I am to have a healthy baby boy to call me "mother". I try to thank God for this blessing each day.

Bible Connection:
Mary's Thoughts about Being a Mother

Mary had found favor with God and would give birth to the Son of the Most High. Mary said, "My soul glorifies the Lord and my spirit rejoices in God my Savior, for He has been mindful of the humble state of His servant. From now on all generations will call me blessed, for the Mighty One has done great things for me – holy is His name." (Luke 1:30-32, 46-49)

Personal Connection
Role #3: Mother

As women, we are reminded of the blessing of being a mother when we gaze into our baby's eyes. As children grow and struggles arise, it becomes harder to remember that blessing. Mary had many struggles as a mother throughout her lifetime; the most difficult one was watching her Son be crucified. Still, she always considered it a blessing to be Jesus' mother. Let's follow Mary's example and think of being a mother as a blessing to treasure. This blessing may bring struggle, but it is often through struggle that the blessing is realized once again.

 A Welcome Retreat

Prayer to Share (with children): *Lord, thank You for my children. It is a blessing to be their mother.*
Question: Do you think of being a mother as a blessing to treasure?
Contemporary Music – *Worship* CD:
  Song Title: *"Breathe"* – Track 7
Traditional Music – *Ryman Gospel Reunion* CD:
  Song Title: *"Turn Your Radio On"* – Track 1

Chapter 12: Day 4
Self-Absorbed Thoughts

> You live with your thoughts –
> so be careful what they are.
> - Eva Arrington

As our puppy Turner watched the car back out of the driveway, he thought, *Everyone is gone. This is what I've been waiting for. They'll never even know.* He leaped off the couch and scampered down the stairs, making a beeline for the kitchen.

Unfortunately, everyone was not gone. As Rich rounded the kitchen corner, he saw Turner straining on his hind legs to reach a bag of chips. After dragging it down to the floor, Turner eased off the chip clip. Without pause, he dove headfirst into the chip bag, noisily chowing down. The only part of his little Pomeranian body that could be seen was his fluffy tail, sticking out of the end of the chip bag.

Rich tweaked Turner's tail, nudging him further into the bag. In shock, Turner shot out of the chip bag. His eyes wildly shifted back and forth, searching for who could have possibly caught him. Little bits of chips were stuck everywhere in his fur, and the grease from the bag had slicked his hair back like Elvis's. He raced away to hide in his kennel, knowing that it would be his home for a while.

Turner's selfish thoughts had gotten him into trouble. He had a terrible stomachache, a greasy hair-do, and a lot of time alone in his kennel. He had to learn that selfish thoughts lead to selfish actions; which in turn, have natural consequences. Turner had to learn this same lesson often.

BIBLE CONNECTION:
A RICH MAN'S SELFISH THOUGHTS

Jesus told this parable: A rich man's crops produced so much grain that he had no place to store it. He was selfish and decided to tear down his barns and build bigger ones. He thought selfishly, *I have plenty of good things laid up for many years. I'll take life easy; eat, drink, and be merry.* God called him a fool and as a consequence demanded his life from him that night. This is how it is for anyone who stores up things for himself but is not rich toward God. (Luke 12:16-21)

PERSONAL CONNECTION
ROLE #4: TEACHER

The rich fool thought only of his own needs and neglected the chance to help others. The consequences for his selfish actions were severe. As teachers of our children, we need to show them selfish thinking is wrong. There will be many opportunities to help our children learn this lesson, since children are naturally selfish. Jesus modeled a different way of thinking, which was servant-like. Let's teach our children to imitate Jesus' kind of thinking rather than the world's. Then, just maybe, we can start to turn this "me-first" thinking world around, one child at a time.

 A WELCOME RETREAT

Prayer to Share (with children): *Lord, please help us to think of others' needs before our own, just like Jesus thought of us first.*
Question: Do your children know that selfish thinking is a bad habit that has consequences?
Contemporary Music – *Worship* CD:
  Song Title: *"Breathe"* – Track 7
Traditional Music – *Ryman Gospel Reunion* CD:
  Song Title: *"Turn Your Radio On"* – Track 1

Chapter 12: Day 5
Reflecting on Thoughts

Role #1: Christian Woman
Spend some time today "listening" to your thoughts. When you have a thoughtless thought, replace it with one that is more in keeping with Jesus' example.

Role #2: Wife
What thoughts do you replay about your husband? Pay attention to the words and actions that follow those thoughts.

Role #3: Mother
Do you sometimes forget that being a mother is a blessing to treasure? To measure its worth, imagine having to give up being a mother, and think what you'd give up instead.

Role #4: Teacher
Nurture unselfish thoughts in your children by modeling them yourself. You might kindly say *You can choose first* or *You can have the last cookie* or *I'll read another book for you* etc.

 A Welcome Retreat

Prayer to Share: *Help my thoughts as a Christian woman, a wife, a mother, and a teacher to reflect Your influence in my life.*
Contemporary Music: *"Breathe"*
  Music Connection: No one can hear all of your thoughts but the Lord. When you worship Him with all of your mind, it shows His presence is alive in you.
Traditional Music: *"Turn Your Radio On"*
  Music Connection: Control your thoughts by staying in touch with God and listening for His call.

The very essence of leadership is that you have to have a vision. It's got to be a vision you articulate clearly and forcefully on every occasion. You can't blow an uncertain trumpet.

– Theodore M. Hesburgh

Prepare Your Heart

Prayer:
*As a Christian woman, a wife, a mother, and a teacher,
I give credit to You for all achievements in my life.*

Role #1: Christian Woman
God Deserves Credit for Achievements

Role #2: Wife
Achieving a Common Direction in Marriage

Role #3: Mother
How to Achieve Success

Role #4: Teacher
The Achievement of "Being Somebody"

Contemporary Music Connection:
"Awesome God"
God used His wisdom and power to create you
and to plan important work for you to do.
If you want to achieve great things in your life,
ask God what He wants you to do…and then do it.

Traditional Music Connection:
"When Jesus Says It's Enough…"
With Jesus by your side, you can achieve almost anything.
Have faith and step out into the storms of life for Him;
He'll be holding your hand.

Chapter 13: Day 1

God Deserves Credit for Achievements

> Think so big that you can't do it alone, so big you can't do it this year, this decade or even in your lifetime. Have a dream worth dreaming, a challenge so big that even credit isn't necessary.
> - Bobb Biehl

I dreamed of being a part of a women's group that loved reading God's word, having good food and hot coffee, and sharing personal struggles and triumphs. The result of that dream was my directing a Coffee Break women's Bible study at our church. Many volunteers needed to be found, so I began calling people that I thought would fit each position. I made announcements in church, and I hung up a volunteer sign, but I found very few people to volunteer.

I couldn't think of anything else to do but begin calling each member of the church personally to ask for help. After calling countless people, and only turning up a few volunteers, I began wondering if this ministry really had God's blessing. That's when I prayed for God to open the hearts and minds of the people that I was about to call, so that <u>He</u> could pick the right people for each of the jobs. God chose two special volunteers that night.

The calling was still a slow process after that, but because I prayed for God to pick the volunteers, I felt a sense of peace with each of their answers. God has filled almost all of the Coffee Break positions now, and His choices have been so wise. He knew exactly who was best for each position all along; I just had to stop trying to do His job, and give Him credit for His wisdom each step of the way.

BIBLE CONNECTION: MIRIAM WANTS MORE CREDIT THAN MOSES

Miriam and Aaron began to talk against Moses. They said, "Has the Lord spoken only through Moses? Hasn't He also spoken through us?" God heard them and came down in a pillar of cloud. He told them He'd personally chosen Moses for this task, knowing he'd be faithful. God asked them why they were not afraid to speak against Moses? God's anger burned, and when the cloud lifted, Miriam was white with leprosy. Moses pleaded for God to heal her, and after seven days, God did. (Numbers 12:1-15)

PERSONAL CONNECTION
ROLE #1: CHRISTIAN WOMAN

Miriam and Aaron got caught up in bickering over who was to receive credit for the work that had been done, but they forgot that God was the One deserving the credit. When we begin to try to achieve things on our own, the Lord will quickly remind us that we can't take credit for His work. As Christian women, let's give credit for all the good things that have been achieved in our lives to our Almighty Lord. All good things come from Him, and there should never be a question to whom credit is due.

    A WELCOME RETREAT

Prayer to Share: *Lord, please use me to do Your work. All credit is due to You for anything positive that is achieved in my life.*
Question: Do you remember to give credit to God for all of His achievements in your life?
Contemporary Music – *Worship* CD:
  Song Title: *"Awesome God"* – Track 10
Traditional Music – *Ryman Gospel Reunion* CD:
  Song Title: *"When Jesus Says It's Enough…"* – Track 7

Chapter 13: Day 2

Achieving A Common Direction in Marriage

> If you don't make a total commitment to whatever you're doing, then you start looking to bail out the first time the boat starts leaking. It's tough enough getting that boat to shore with everybody rowing, let alone when a guy stands up and starts putting his life jacket on.
> - Lou Holtz

Rich and I had been engaged for three months when we went on a vacation with my parents to Yellowstone Park. We saw Old Faithful, a great rodeo, and wildlife galore. On the way to Jackson Hole, we passed billboards picturing screaming people barreling through wild rapids, and after about the second billboard, Rich became convinced he and I needed to brave the rapids too. I was less than enthused - I mean the people were screaming, and they looked positively terrified. However, we'd done all of the tourist things I'd wanted to do, so I felt like I owed it to him to get into the raft.

About 10 people got into the raft that day. The men looked elated, and the women looked like they would rather be doing almost anything else than getting into that raft. The water seemed deceivingly calm at first, but it wasn't long before we all looked just like the people we'd seen on the billboard – screaming and positively terrified as we barreled through gushing waterfalls and wild rapids.

The funny thing was I loved every single minute of it. From the chuckle I had when Rich fell out of the raft, to the majestic eagles we saw, it was an amazing ride. Just think what I would have missed if I'd never gotten on the boat!

BIBLE CONNECTION: NOAH'S WIFE GETS ON THE BOAT

God established a covenant with Noah. When Noah turned six hundred years old, the springs of the great deep burst forth, and the floodgates of the heavens opened. Noah and his sons, along with his wife and his sons' wives, trusted God and obediently got in the ark. When Noah turned six hundred one, the water dried up, and God told Noah to come out of the ark with his wife, and his sons, and their wives. (Genesis 6:18; 7:11-13; 8:13-16)

PERSONAL CONNECTION
ROLE #2: WIFE

Noah's wife must have had some reservations about the building of that colossal ark, but all men have some sort of "project" going on, so she probably viewed it like we do when our husbands head to the garage or disappear in the yard. The true test of commitment was getting on the boat and weathering the storm with Noah. As wives, sometimes the greatest achievement in our marriage will be simply getting on board with our husband and being willing to head in the direction he's aiming. It may take courage, but it could be the most memorable ride of our life!

 A WELCOME RETREAT

Prayer to Share (with husband): *I am committed to my husband, and I'll go where he leads, as long as You are leading him.*
Question: Are you willing to achieve true commitment in your marriage by following where your husband leads?
Contemporary Music – *Worship* CD:
  Song Title: *"Awesome God"* – Track 10
Traditional Music – *Ryman Gospel Reunion* CD:
  Song Title: *"When Jesus Says It's Enough…"* – Track 7

CHAPTER 13: DAY 3

How to Achieve Success

> People never improve unless they look to some standard or example higher and better than themselves.
> - Tryon Edwards

What is success? When I was very young, success was a perfect sunny day spent playing outside with my sisters, cats, and dog. In elementary school, success was a good report card, a few nice friends, invitations to birthday parties, and a valentine from everyone in the class. In middle school, success was getting good grades, remembering the combination to my locker, getting asked to dance, and getting teased fewer times than someone else.

In high school, success was scoring the most steals in a basketball game, winning first chair in band, dating a "popular" boy, being invited to parties, being skinny enough to fit into a single-digit size, and earning decent grades. In college, success was joining a sorority, receiving excellent grades, getting the lead role in a musical, dating someone "important", and not gaining the "freshman 15".

Most of the things on those "success" lists seem pretty shallow now. Blessedly, God has helped me to redefine my definition of success, both for myself and for my children. As a mother, if I live my life for God and teach my children to do the same, I'd consider that a success. If my sons become strong Christians, good providers, and loving husbands and fathers, I'd consider that to be a success. I've learned the hard way that true success is based on Scripture and comes from having a right relationship with God. I pray my children define success that way sooner than I did.

BIBLE CONNECTION:
HOW KING SISERA'S MOTHER RATED SUCCESS

King Sisera had nine hundred iron chariots, and he had cruelly oppressed the Israelites for twenty years. The Lord allowed Sisera to be killed by a woman as he slept. Meanwhile, Sisera's mother waited for him. As she peered through the window behind the lattice, she cried out, "Why is my son's chariot so long in coming?" The wisest of her ladies said he was probably finding and dividing the spoils of war. As King Sisera's mother imagined the colorful and highly embroidered garments she'd receive, her concern faded away. (Judges 4:2-3, 21; 5:28-30)

PERSONAL CONNECTION
ROLE #3: MOTHER

King Sisera's mother valued material things, and she seemed to think it was an achievement to acquire them by force. It's not surprising then that her son owned nine hundred chariots and oppressed the Israelites with his power. As mothers, we hope our children will achieve more success than we did, we hope they don't make the same mistakes we did, but maybe our greatest hope should be that they learn to measure achievement by God's standards.

 ## A WELCOME RETREAT

Prayer to Share (with children): *Lord, help my children to know that the greatest achievement is to live life for You.*
Question: How would your children say you measure achievement?
Contemporary Music – *Worship* CD:
  Song Title: *"Awesome God"* – Track 10
Traditional Music – *Ryman Gospel Reunion* CD:
  Song Title: *"When Jesus Says It's Enough…"* – Track 7

Chapter 13: Day 4

The Achievement of "Being Somebody"

> I have always wanted to be somebody,
> but I see now I should have been more specific.
> - Lily Tomlin

I made it a point to try to be nice to everyone in high school. I wasn't part of the "popular crowd", but I did get along with almost everyone – except for a few girls who always disliked me with a passion. Every time I received any type of honor, they were furious. I didn't get into wearing certain clothes or being friends with certain people, and I think they couldn't understand why I was chosen for things like prom bouncer, sweetheart queen, or class officer. To be honest, I couldn't understand it either.

The biggest surprise came during my senior year when I was nominated for homecoming queen. Those girls were livid because they weren't nominated, and they actually had the principal recount the votes. At the homecoming ceremony, they glared angrily at me, and I could see how much they coveted my seat on the stage. When I wasn't chosen as queen, they turned their anger on the girl who was crowned. She'd only attended our high school for a year, and they argued that she should have attended high school longer to be queen.

When we get caught up in trying to "be somebody", we should stop and remember we are somebody already. God created each of us to be unique, and we each have a special purpose to fulfill for Him. Sitting in a certain seat isn't going to make us "be somebody", but being somebody for God will set us apart in exactly the way God intended.

BIBLE CONNECTION: GUESTS COVET HONORED WEDDING SEATS

When Jesus noticed the guests picked to sit in the places of honor at the table, He told them this parable: When someone invites you to a wedding feast, do not take the place of honor, for a person more distinguished than you may have been invited. If so, the host who invited you will come and tell you to give your seat to that person. Then, humiliated, you will have to take the least important place. But when you are invited, take the lowest place, so that when your host comes, he will tell you to move up to a better place. Then you will be honored in the presence of all your fellow guests. (Luke 14:7-10)

PERSONAL CONNECTION
ROLE #4: TEACHER

Each of us aspires to achieve certain things in our lives, but when we only care about winning and losing, nothing can be gained. We need to teach our children that true achievement can't be measured by votes, scores, income, or trophies. It can only be measured by God. When your children want to "be somebody", remind them that God made them somebody the day He created them.

 A WELCOME RETREAT

Prayer to Share (with children): *Lord, my children don't have to try to "be somebody" because they already are in Your eyes.*
Question: Do your children know the only "somebody" they need to be is the somebody God wants them to be?
Contemporary Music – *Worship* CD:
 Song Title: *"Awesome God"* – Track 10
Traditional Music – *Ryman Gospel Reunion* CD:
 Song Title: *"When Jesus Says It's Enough…"* – Track 7

Chapter 13: Day 5

Reflecting on Achievement

Role #1: Christian Woman
What do you dream of achieving for God? Ask God to use you to do His work, and thank Him when He does.

Role #2: Wife
Are you and your husband in the same boat, rowing in the same direction? Together, pray for God's direction in your life, and get ready to row…in unison.

Role #3: Mother
What do you hope your children achieve in their lifetime? The greatest achievement is to live their life for God.

Role #4: Teacher
Ask your children who they would want to be like and why. Respond suitably, and teach them that God already made them somebody special the day He created them.

 A Welcome Retreat

Prayer to Share: *As a Christian woman, a wife, a mother, and a teacher, I give credit to You for all achievements in my life.*
Contemporary Music: *"Awesome God"*
  Music Connection: God used His wisdom and power to create you and to plan important work for you to do. If you want to achieve great things in your life, ask God what He wants you to do…and then do it.
Traditional Music: *"When Jesus Says Its Enough…"*
  Music Connection: With Jesus by your side, you can achieve almost anything. Have faith and step out into the storms of life for Him; He'll be holding your hand.

The important thing is to start,
to lay a plan and then follow it
step-by-step, no matter
how small or large each step
by itself may seem.

- Robert Louis Stevenson

Prepare Your Heart

Prayer:
Lord, help me to organize my roles of Christian woman, wife, mother, and teacher so my entire life reflects You.

Role #1: Christian Woman
Little Changes Make Big Differences

Role #2: Wife
Be Deliberate in Your Actions

Role #3: Mother
Planning to Protect Our Children

Role #4: Teacher
It's Not Enough Just to Want Something

Contemporary Music Connection:
"More Love, More Power"
When you organize your life to have more of God in it, you will feel more of His love and power because He is at the center of your life.

Traditional Music Connection:
"I Need You"
Realize that you need God as much as flowers require sunshine and trees depend on rain, and make an effort to organize all of your life around Him.

Chapter 14: Day 1

Little Changes Make Big Differences

> We must not ... ignore the small daily differences
> we can make which, over time, add up to
> big differences that we often cannot foresee.
> - Marian Write Edelman

When I first began staying home with my children, I took great joy in donning my comfortable sweat outfits, wearing no make-up, and letting my wet hair air-dry. Several years into this routine, I began to avoid looking at myself in the mirror, and the ring of the doorbell brought great distress. If I had to go out to get the mail, I became a "little streak of sweat suit" as I sprinted to and from the mailbox, dreading the thought of the neighbors catching a glimpse of me. When Rich came home, I felt like a "blob of sweat suit" as he gave me a hug dressed in his handsome work attire.

My sister Carrie was my "fellow sweat suit wearer". When we traveled to book fairs together, our "sweat suit uniforms" made us feel out of place eating at nicer restaurants, and as she and I downed another fast food burger, we vowed it was time for a change. We hit an outlet mall on the way home and bought enough jean skirt outfits to wear for a week. We made an organized plan to wear our skirts every day for a month, paint our toenails, do our hair, and wear make-up. We did not tell anyone about our plans.

Throughout the month, we began to see a difference in the way we were treated. Men got the door for us, called us "ladies", and helped us carry things. Our children told us we looked pretty, and our husbands commented on our happier disposition. That was about a year ago, and we've been wearing our skirts ever since. Taking better care of myself has made me feel like a woman again. Sometimes feeling good about being a woman comes down to the little things. Changing those little things, one step at a time, can make a big difference in the overall way we feel.

Bible Connection:
Wise Hearted Women Get Organized

The tabernacle needed to be adorned, so every skilled woman spun blue, purple or scarlet fine linen. Then, all the women who were willing and had the skill to do so spun goat's hair to make a beautiful contribution of cloth to the tabernacle. (Exodus 35:25-26)

Personal Connection
Role #1: Christian Woman

Women often have a flair for organizing things while still paying attention to the colorful details. As Christian women, people should be able to see femininity in us. Getting in touch with our feminine side is one way to get in touch with the way God intended us to be. Small steps make big differences, and a little organization goes a long way. If need be, take a step to be more feminine today.

 A Welcome Retreat

Prayer to Share: *Lord, help me to be the feminine woman You created me to be. Help me not to get caught up in the worldly trend of being more unisex.*
Question: How are you in touch with your feminine side?
Contemporary Music – ***Worship*** **CD:**
  Song Title: *"More Love, More Power"* – Track 11
Traditional Music – ***Ryman Gospel Reunion*** **CD:**
  Song Title: *"I Need You"* – Track 15

Chapter 14: Day 2

Be Deliberate in Your Actions

> Know what you want to do, hold the thought firmly,
> and do every day what should be done, and
> every sunset will see you that much nearer the goal.
> - Elbert Hubbard

My mother's holiday dinners have beautiful table settings and mouth-watering food served at exactly the right time. I haven't had a holiday dinner yet, but I have made dinner for my sons' birthday parties. We are blessed to have a lot of family living near us, so we usually serve about 20-25 people. Since we have the parties on Sundays after church (since that's when people can come), we've tried various time-saving tactics. I would not advise you to try these.

One year I made different kinds of soup the night before the party. On the party day, I heated each person's bowl of soup separately in the microwave. No one ate at the same time, and it took forever. Another year, I decided to serve store-bought lasagna. I forgot to double the baking time since I was preparing two lasagnas, and they were frozen when we were supposed to begin eating. One year I used time bake for the ham. I forgot to change the oven clock after daylight savings time, and again, the meal was cold.

Out of necessity, we've made a few changes. Rich now makes a turkey or ham, and I make everything else. We also bring tables in the garage and decorate it all the night before. On the party day, we eat in the garage and come inside for cake and visiting. Deciding what each of us is best at doing has helped Rich and I become organized, and in about ten years I may be ready to cook for the holidays.

BIBLE CONNECTION: ABIGAIL IS DELIBERATE IN HER ACTIONS

Abigail was an intelligent and beautiful woman. Her husband, Nabal, was a wealthy man, but he was often surly. David protected Nabal's flocks in the midst of a battle, and then he asked Nabal to share some food and supplies with him. Nabal refused, and David was so insulted that he and his men began putting on their swords. Abigail quickly made a plan to solve the problem. She took bread, wine, sheep, grain, raisins, and figs and brought them to David. David told Abigail, "Praise be to the Lord who has sent you to meet me. May you be blessed for your good judgment for stopping any bloodshed." (I Samuel 25:3-19, 32-33)

PERSONAL CONNECTION
ROLE #2: WIFE

Nabal was a businessman, and in his mind it made no sense to help David, even though David had helped him. Abigail, on the other hand, knew David was a godly man, and she wasted no time getting organized to help him. As wives, it's a good idea to be aware of what we do best, and what our husbands do best. Then, we can work together in an organized way that makes the best of any situation.

 A WELCOME RETREAT

Prayer to Share (with husband): *Lord, please help my husband and I to be organized in working together.*
Question: Do you and your husband spend time organizing plans that utilize each of you the best?
Contemporary Music – *Worship* CD:
  Song Title: *"More Love, More Power"* – Track 11
Traditional Music – *Ryman Gospel Reunion* CD:
  Song Title: *"I Need You"* – Track 15

Chapter 14: Day 3

Planning to Protect Our Children

> A sheltered life can be a daring life as well.
> For all serious daring starts from within.
> - Eudora Welty

It was my first interview for a teaching job, and I was told to wait in the office. I'd only just sat down when a girl rushed in, sobbing and holding her arm. Blood was pouring out of a deep, dark line at the center of a cut in her arm. Another girl with a satisfied smirk on her face sauntered in right behind her. She laughingly said, "You'd better not rat on me." The girl that was crying adamantly promised she wouldn't, and the principal called her into the office.

Moments later, the principal motioned me into her office and explained the "cool thing to do" was to sharpen a pencil, stab it into a person, and break it off. She'd hardly finished speaking when the secretary interrupted to ask for assistance. As we came out, I saw another pair of students. Again, one of the boys was bleeding, and another boy sat across from him, laughing and pointing at him. After the principal had talked with them, she explained that much of her day was spent dealing with altercations such as these.

Experiences such as these are not "rites of passage", and they should not be "part of growing up". Seeing appalling things such as these makes me want to protect my children. Some people may say I shelter my children too much. To them I say, you have no idea what goes on at schools – even *nice* schools. The repercussions of protecting my children are far less dangerous than the repercussions of *not* protecting them. If the worst thing that happens to my children is being "sheltered", I'll be a very content mother.

Bible Connection:
Jehosheba Plans to Save Joash's Life

Athaliah wanted to rule Judah, so she began to destroy the royal family. But, Jehosheba, who was an aunt of the royal family, daringly stole baby Joash away and put him and his nurse in a bedroom to hide him from Athaliah. After that, he led a sheltered life, hidden at the temple of the Lord for six more years while Athaliah ruled the land. In the seventh year, Joash was brought out from hiding and crowned king, and then Athaliah was put to death. (II Kings 11:1-16)

Personal Connection
Role #3: Mother

When Athaliah threatened Joash, Jehosheba didn't stick around to reason with her. Instead, she removed Joash from the situation completely. As mothers, let's plan to protect our children from the "Athaliahs" of this world. Sheltering our children a little too much probably isn't the worst thing we can do. In fact, just like in Joash's case, it may turn out to be the very best thing we ever did.

 A Welcome Retreat

Prayer to Share (with children): *Lord, help me to protect my children by removing them from negative settings as much as possible.*
Question: How are you protecting your children from the "Athaliahs" of this world?
Contemporary Music – ***Worship*** **CD:**
  Song Title: *"More Love, More Power"* – Track 11
Traditional Music – ***Ryman Gospel Reunion*** **CD:**
  Song Title: *"I Need You"* – Track 15

Chapter 14: Day 4

It's Not Enough Just to Want Something

> Before you begin a thing remind yourself that difficulties and delays quite impossible to foresee are ahead…You can only see one thing clearly, and that is your goal. Form a mental vision of that and cling to it through thick and thin.
> - Kathleen Norris

Watching my sisters homeschool their children helped me visualize how great it would be to homeschool our children. However, my husband Rich did not share this vision, so I began praying for God's guidance, and I asked Rich to pray too. Wyatt was only 2 ½ years old, so to get an idea of what homeschooling would be like, I began doing some informal learning activities with him each day. By the time he was 3 ½ , I began using my sister's preschool program <u>Little Hands to Heaven</u>. From the moment we started, I was hooked, and so was he. A year later, we began <u>Little Hearts for His Glory</u> (the follow-up to the preschool program).

I loved the program, and there is nothing more exciting than teaching your own child to read! However, as I looked ahead to the next year, I began worrying about having enough time to homeschool. I was still working part-time from my home 4 hours a day as an on-line tutor, and our other son Riley was 15 months old. Rich was more supportive of homeschooling, but he didn't want to give up my income. I prayed for God to tell us what to do.

The next week, I got an email from my employer that said my income would be reduced by 40% due to budget cuts. That same week, Rich received a raise at work. This was an answer to prayer because I was able to quit my job and have more time to homeschool without lowering our income. I'm sure there will be more setbacks along the way, but by homeschooling, we are laying the foundation that the rest of our children's lives will be built upon, and whatever the setbacks are, that's a building project worth finishing.

Bible Connection: A Tower Builder Gets Organized

Jesus told this parable: Suppose one of you wants to build a tower. Will he not first sit down and estimate the cost to see if he has enough money to complete it? For if he lays the foundation and is not able to finish it, everyone who sees it will ridicule him, saying 'This fellow began to build and was not able to finish'. (Luke 14:28-30)

Personal Connection Role #4: Teacher

Homeschooling is as big of a project as building a tower, and it's probably an even more important one because it involves building the character and minds of our children. As teachers of our children, let's commit to finishing the project of homeschooling, even if unforeseen setbacks arise.

 A Welcome Retreat

Prayer to Share (with children): *Lord, help our homeschooling to bring You glory. Help us to be focused even through setbacks.*
Question: How committed are you to homeschooling your children in a godly manner?
Contemporary Music – ***Worship*** **CD:**
 Song Title: *"More Love, More Power"* – Track 11
Traditional Music – ***Ryman Gospel Reunion*** **CD:**
 Song Title: *"I Need You"* – Track 15

# Chapter 14: Day 5
Reflecting on Organization

Role #1: Christian Woman
Do you take time for things that make you the feminine woman God intended you to be? If you've been neglecting your feminine side, consider making a little change today.

Role #2: Wife
Is there a recurring problem that your husband and you could be more organized in addressing? Take time to divvy out duties and organize a plan together.

Role #3: Mother
What situations seem to threaten your children's well-being? Weigh the benefits with the costs and make organized decisions about what your children do outside your home.

Role #4: Teacher
Plan on there being setbacks in teaching your children. Plan on God to help you overcome them.

 A Welcome Retreat

Prayer to Share: *Lord, help me to organize my roles of Christian woman, wife, mother, and teacher so my entire life reflects You.*

Contemporary Music: *"More Love, More Power"*
  Music Connection: When you organize your life to have more of God in it, you will feel more of His love and power because He is at the center of your life.

Traditional Music: *"I Need You"*
  Music Connection: Realize that you need God as much as flowers require sunshine and trees depend on rain, and make an effort to organize all of your life around Him.

Peace rules the day
when Christ rules the mind.

– Anonymous

Prepare Your Heart

Prayer:
As a Christian woman, a wife, a mother, and a teacher help me have a calm disposition instead of an angry one.

Role #1: Christian Woman
Why Is This Happening?

Role #2: Wife
Being Calm When a Mistake Has Been Made

Role #3: Mother
When Children Are Wayward

Role #4: Teacher
Habits Are Hard to Break

Contemporary Music Connection:
"Agnus Dei"
The Lord reigns over all of creation. When
He reigns in your heart, you can depend on Him
to ease your anger and bring you peace
in even the most trying situations.

Traditional Music Connection:
"The Unclouded Day"
Some of your days on earth will be stormy, but your days
in heaven will be free from storms, sorrows, and tears.
This hope for tomorrow can bring you peace today
if you only look to God for help.

Chapter 15: Day 1

Why Is This Happening?

> Peace comes not from the absence of conflict in life but from the ability to cope with it.
> - Anonymous

My dad is a big, strong man, and he's hardly ever been sick a day in his life. That's why I could hardly believe it when my sister Carrie called to tell me Dad was in an ambulance headed for the hospital because he was having heart problems. As Carrie and I hurriedly made our way to the hospital, a thousand thoughts rushed through my mind. *Was he having a heart attack? Would I be able to talk to him again? Did he know how much I loved him? Why was this happening?!?*

My mom, Carrie, and I spent a long fitful night trying to sleep on hospital chairs. Finally, in the wee hours of the morning, the doctor told us Dad did have a silent heart attack, and an angioplasty would be necessary to repair the damage. The doctor showed us Dad's x-rays and pointed to a large, dark shadow. He told us that this shadow was more of a concern than the heart attack. It was an abdominal aneurysm, and it could kill my dad instantly if it burst.

It suddenly occurred to me that we never would have known about the aneurysm if Dad hadn't had a heart attack. Then I understood why this had happened, and I had another reason to thank God for His perfect plan. My dad's angioplasty went well, and a month later he had stints put in to fix his aneurysm. That entire time my dad had a calmness about him that gave all of us a sense of peace. My dad's peace came from his faith in God, and depending on God allowed all of us to cope with the conflict better.

Bible Connection:
A Sick Woman Finds Peace in Jesus

A woman had been bleeding for twelve years. When she heard about Jesus, she thought, *If I just touch His cloak, I know I will be healed.* So, she came up behind Jesus in the crowd and touched His cloak. Immediately her bleeding stopped, and she felt her body freed from her suffering. Jesus realized that power had gone out from Him, and He asked the crowd who had touched Him. The woman fell at His feet and told Him the whole truth. Jesus said, "Take heart, daughter, your faith has healed you." (Mark 5:25-34)

Personal Connection
Role #1: Christian Woman

This woman had endured twelve years of severe health problems. Scripture tells us doctors had been unable to help her, and all of her money had been spent trying to find a cure. As it turned out, the cure was a spiritually ordained meeting with Jesus, and her faith in Him was all it took to heal her. As Christian women, when we think, *Why is this happening?*, let's remember God has the best plan for us. Our faith in God certainly doesn't mean our lives won't have conflict, but it can give us the peace to cope with it.

 A Welcome Retreat

Prayer to Share: *Lord, when I don't understand why something is happening help my faith in You to give me peace through the conflict.*
Question: When you wonder why something is happening, do you depend on your faith in God to bring you peace?
Contemporary Music – *Worship* CD:
  Song Title: *"Agnus Dei"* – Track 9
Traditional Music – *Ryman Gospel Reunion* CD:
  Song Title: *"The Unclouded Day"* – Track 2

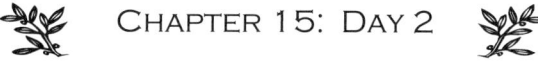

Chapter 15: Day 2

Being Calm When a Mistake Has Been Made

> The worst-tempered people I ever met
> were people who knew they were wrong.
> - Wilson Mizner

It was the 40th wedding anniversary of Rich's parents, and a big celebration was planned. No one attending the celebration had small children, except us. So, we decided to take the kids for the first several hours and have a babysitter watch them at a friend's house for the rest of the evening.

When we got there, Riley raced up and down the aisles and finally chose a chair by a bowl of candy hearts. He had eaten most of them by the time I figured out Rich wasn't watching him, and Rich figured out I wasn't watching him. Riley screamed as we put him in the high chair and began chanting, *All done! All done!* before we even gave him his food. (Who needs food, when you've got candy hearts?)

Since Riley wouldn't eat, we made the mistake of turning him loose. He raced into the restaurant, ran into a waiter, hid under a table, and had to be dragged out. He escaped again only to barrel into a lady with a walker. That was when I yelled for Rich, and we dashed for the door, with Riley screaming the entire way out. As we drove to our friend's house, Rich and I each blamed one another for our predicament. Later, we decided we'd misjudged Riley's capability to handle that situation. In hindsight, our expectations for our little Riley weren't in keeping with his maturity level. The next time Rich and I make a mistake together, we hope to spend less time blaming each other, and more time deciding what to do differently in the future.

Bible Connection:
Joseph and Mary Are Mistakenly Angry

Jesus was twelve years old when Joseph and Mary took Him to the Passover Feast at the temple in Jerusalem. After it was over, Jesus stayed behind without them knowing it. Mary and Joseph searched for three days before they found Him talking with the teachers back at the temple. Mary said, "Son, why have You treated us like this? Your father and I have been anxiously searching for You."

Jesus said, "Why were you searching for Me? Didn't you know I had to be in My Father's house?" (Luke 2:41-49)

Personal Connection
Role #2: Wife

Joseph and Mary became upset with Jesus because they were worried about Him, and they didn't understand His actions. However, Jesus had simply chosen to be obedient to His heavenly Father, instead of His earthly father. Quite the opposite of our little Riley, Jesus proved Himself to be more mature than His parents had anticipated. In times when we feel like placing blame on those closest to us, it's worthwhile to spend less time blaming each other, and more time deciding what to do differently in the future.

 A Welcome Retreat

Prayer to Share (with husband): *Lord, help my husband and I to spend less time placing blame and more time solving problems.*
Question: Are you and your husband quick to blame one another when things go wrong?
Contemporary Music – *Worship* CD:
  Song Title: *"Agnus Dei"* – Track 9
Traditional Music – *Ryman Gospel Reunion* CD:
  Song Title: *"The Unclouded Day"* – Track 2

Chapter 15: Day 3

When Children Are Wayward

> Gentle words fall lightly, but they have great weight.
> - Croft M. Pentz

Our son Wyatt tries to listen most of the time, but he's had some memorable moments of immaturity. For example, Wyatt was about 3 years old when we had our second son, Riley. We talked a lot about how important it would be for him to love and care for his little brother. A few weeks after we brought Riley home, I asked Wyatt what he thought of Riley. Wyatt said, "He's o.k., but could he go back soon?" This made perfect sense to a 3 year old.

One day I told Wyatt to pick up the toys in the backyard after he had finished swimming. A few minutes later, I looked out the window to see Wyatt carrying two beach balls to the toy box. He was certainly putting the toys away, but he was also completely naked. As I rushed out to ask him what he was doing, he told me he was putting the toys away. When I asked him why he took off his swim trunks, he said he was hot. This made perfect sense to a 4 year old.

Another time I told Wyatt our neighbor was bringing him a birthday treat. I told him to thank her when she gave it to him. When she brought a stuffed toy, Wyatt said nothing. When I asked him why he hadn't thanked her, he said he was still waiting for the "treat". This made perfect sense to a 5 year old. Sometimes Wyatt does **exactly** what I ask him to, and sometimes he doesn't. Other times he's just not mature enough to understand. When my children do things that anger me, I've found gentle words spoken firmly have a longer lasting effect than angry words spoken carelessly.

BIBLE CONNECTION:
SAMSON'S WAYWARDNESS UPSETS HIS MOTHER

After an angel spoke to Samson's mother, she listened to his message and did not drink wine or eat anything unclean during her pregnancy. She also made sure Samson's hair was never cut. Years later, Samson told his parents he'd seen a Philistine woman he wanted for his wife. His parents did not want him to marry her because she did not believe in God. Even though Samson's mother made sure she followed all of God's directions, she gave in, and let Samson marry the Philistine woman. (Judges 13:7-10; 14:1-3)

PERSONAL CONNECTION
ROLE #3: MOTHER

Many times, Samson chose to be with women who did not believe in God. Delilah, the last woman he chose, betrayed him and cost him his life. As mothers, we need to persevere when our children are wayward. We can consider whether the child knowingly disobeyed or was too immature to know he did. Either way, when reproof is needed, it will be better received if it is given in a loving, firm way, instead of in an angry, irrational outburst.

 A WELCOME RETREAT

Prayer to Share (with children): *Lord, when my children are wayward, help me to be loving and firm even if I feel angry inside.*
Question: How do you feel after you've lost control and gotten angry with your children?
Contemporary Music – *Worship* CD:
  Song Title: *"Agnus Dei"* – Track 9
Traditional Music – *Ryman Gospel Reunion* CD:
  Song Title: *"The Unclouded Day"* – Track 2

Chapter 15: Day 4

Habits Are Hard to Break

> A habit is something you can do without thinking – which is why most of us have so many of them.
> - Frank A. Clark

When I was a little girl, I spent long hours tending to our outdoor cats. When a few cats had eye infections, I convinced Dad to get me ointment for them. Then, I proceeded to wash their eyes with a warm washcloth and put on the ointment. This would have been a good thing had the perfectionist side of me not kicked in. Instead of putting the ointment on the few cats with infected eyes, I put it on ALL of the cats (which numbered around 40 since I also fed every stray cat that came our way). Thanks to my "help", ALL forty cats had eye infections.

When I grew a little older, I joined 4-H. I usually did 30-40 projects, and I wanted to receive the highest scores on all of them. One time, as we were loading our projects into our car, our cats ate a few of my cookies (probably to pay me back for the "eye treatment"). I had to substitute some misshapen cookies, and the perfectionist in me was very disappointed at the thought of receiving a lower ribbon. When I still got a blue ribbon, I thought I didn't deserve it.

The perfectionist in me is something I still battle. I have to make a concentrated effort not to be a perfectionist. It seems that behind many bad habits are good intentions, which makes them harder to identify. When I do identify a bad habit of mine, I depend on the Lord to help me fix it – sometimes I ask for His help again…and again…and again.

BIBLE CONNECTION:
JUST WHEN YOU THINK YOU'VE KICKED A HABIT

Jesus told this parable: When an evil spirit comes out of a man, it seeks rest, but cannot find it. So it returns, but when it does, it finds things swept clean and put in order. Then it takes with it seven other spirits, more wicked than itself, and they go in and live there. The final condition of that man is even worse than the first. (Matthew 12:43-45)

PERSONAL CONNECTION
ROLE #4: TEACHER

The man in this parable got rid of one bad "habit" only to have it return and bring with it many more bad "habits". Unfortunately, our children often learn all of our habits – both the good and the bad. I can see the perfectionist in me coming out in my son when he does things like unload my Tupperware drawer to put it all back in "perfectly", or when he wants to write or read "perfectly". As teachers of our children, let's be aware of the habits we are teaching – both the good and the bad. A *good* thing to remember is that sometimes the best way to stop a bad habit in our children is to stop it first in ourselves. A *perfect* thing to remember is to call on the only Perfect One for help.

 A WELCOME RETREAT

Prayer to Share (with children): *Lord, help me be aware of my bad habits, and then help me put an end to them.*

Question: What bad habits do you see in your children that may have been learned from you?

Contemporary Music – *Worship* CD:
  Song Title: *"Agnus Dei"* – Track 9

Traditional Music – *Ryman Gospel Reunion* CD:
  Song Title: *"The Unclouded Day"* – Track 2

Chapter 15: Day 5

Reflecting on Anger

Role #1: Christian Woman
What conflict in your life is causing you to think *Why is this happening?* Pray for God to give you a peace about it.

Role #2: Wife
When is the last time you lashed out at your husband? Looking back, how could you have responded more calmly?

Role #3: Mother
Think of a time you have gotten angry with your children. How could you have responded in a firmer, calmer way? Try that response the next time you feel your anger rising.

Role #4: Teacher
Talk to your children about bad habits. Have each person pick a bad habit to work on, and pray for God's help.

A Welcome Retreat

Prayer to Share: *As a Christian woman, a wife, a mother, and a teacher, help me to have a calm disposition instead of an angry one.*

Contemporary Music: *"Agnus Dei"*
  Music Connection: The Lord reigns over all of creation. When He reigns in your heart, you can depend on Him to ease your anger and bring you peace in even the most trying situations.

Traditional Music: *"The Unclouded Day"*
  Music Connection: Some of your days on earth will be stormy, but your days in heaven will be free from storms, sorrows, and tears. This hope for tomorrow can bring you peace today if you only look to God for help.

Prepare Your Heart

Prayer:
Lord, help me to show more love as a Christian woman, a wife, a mother, and a teacher.

Role #1: Christian Woman
Loving Our Father, with All of Our Heart

Role #2: Wife
Proof of Love

Role #3: Mother
A Mother's Love

Role #4: Teacher
Lasting Love

Contemporary Music Connection:
"Open the Eyes of My Heart"
When you open your heart and mind, you can see God at work in your life. God loves you more than anything. He wants to pour out His love on you.

Traditional Music Connection:
"Out of His Great Love"
No one has a greater love for you than God does. Your salvation is possible only because of His great love. Remember to give Him your love in return. It's the least He deserves for being a loving God!

Chapter 16: Day 1

Loving Our Father, with All of Our Heart

> To believe in God's love is to believe that He's passionately interested in each of us personally and continually.
> - Louis Evely

<u>To Hear My Daddy Pray</u>
(Cindy, my sister, wrote this when she was 17 years old. This poem shows why we love our father, with all of our hearts.)

We're around the breakfast table
as the winter morning dawns.
Mom's in her robe, Dad in his jeans
we girls still in our nightgowns.
Dad is joking, we girls are grumbling
then Mom says, "Shall we pray?"
We look at each other guiltily
Mom starts in her soft, gentle way.
Next it is my turn, then the girls,
we stumble through sincerely,
we pray from our hearts even though
we are tired and it is early.
Julie finishes, and then, oh and then,
it's my Daddy's turn to pray.
We all sit straighter, Dad begins,
"Our Heavenly Father," we hear him say.
His voice is loud and strong
almost booming, yet so kind;
in faith he thanks God for the crop
which has not yet all been combined.
He prays with somber graveness
So clearly with thankfulness
he remembers the sick, the hungry, the lost,
asks the Father to richly bless.
Then I hear that humble farmer's voice

pray for each of his daughters
Tears light my eyes, and love and faith
seem to be all that matters.
Cuz no preacher's prayer can move me
like my Daddy's prayer can when he prays.
His words and ways of talking to God
will be written on my heart always.

BIBLE CONNECTION:
MARY OF BETHANY SHOWS HER LOVE

Mary loved Jesus so much that she poured expensive perfume on His feet and then wiped it with her hair. One of the disciples objected, but Jesus said, "Leave her alone. It was intended, that she should save this perfume for the day of my burial. You will always have the poor among you, but you will not always have me." (John 12:3-8)

PERSONAL CONNECTION
ROLE #1: CHRISTIAN WOMAN

Mary loved Jesus with all of her heart. Her relationship with Him was deep and personal. My sisters and I have that kind of relationship with our dad, and our dad has that kind of relationship with God. As Christian women, we need to have a deep love for our Heavenly Father. We need to love Him in a way that is written on our hearts, always.

 A WELCOME RETREAT

Prayer to Share: *I love you more than anything, Lord!*
Question: Can your heavenly Father tell by your thoughts and actions that He's most important in your life?
Contemporary Music – *Worship* CD:
  Song Title: *"Open the Eyes of My Heart"* – Track 5
Traditional Music – *Ryman Gospel Reunion* CD:
  Song Title: *"Out of His Great Love"* – Track 9

Chapter 16: Day 2

Proof of Love

> The most important thing a father can do
> for his children is to love their mother.
> - Theodore M. Hesburgh

"You never tell me that you love me, unless I say it first," I said. "And when was the last time you gave me roses or asked me out on a date? Do you really love me anymore?"

"Of course I love you!" Rich said. "I've already told you I love you anyway, so why do I need to keep saying it? We're married. Isn't that proof enough for you?"

We each escaped to our separate corners of the house for some needed space. After we'd both calmed down, I asked him how he thought he showed me that he loved me.

He told me that he filled my car with gas and took excellent care of it, so it would be safe for me to drive. He also mentioned working hard at his job to support our family, keeping the garage clean, balancing the checkbook, mowing the lawn, and scooping the snow.

I began to see a pattern in Rich's answers. He shows his love for me by the work he does. On the other hand, I show my love for him by spending time with him and by saying loving things.

Since then, we have both come to realize that the way we show our love is not as important as the fact that we do actually love each other. Even though we show love in different ways, our children can still tell that we love each other deeply. If that's enough proof of love for them, then sometimes, it needs to be enough proof for us too.

BIBLE CONNECTION:
JACOB WORKS TO PROVE HIS LOVE

Jacob fell in love with Rachel. He told her father Laban, "I love your daughter Rachel so much that I'll work for you for seven years in return for her hand in marriage." Laban agreed to these terms, but after seven years of work, Laban deceived Jacob, and gave his daughter Leah to him instead. Laban told Jacob he could still wed Rachel if he worked another seven years. So Jacob worked seven more years, and Rachel became his wife too. (Genesis 29:18-30)

PERSONAL CONNECTION
ROLE #2: WIFE

Jacob worked fourteen years to have Rachel be his wife. Jacob's love for Rachel was obvious by the work he was willing to do for her. Our husbands prove their love for us each day by the work that they do. As wives, we need to remember that this is one way of showing love, and some of the time, this needs to be enough.

A WELCOME RETREAT

Prayer to Share (with husband): *Thank you for a husband that works hard to provide for our family. I love him so much!*
Question: Does your husband know how much you love him, and that you appreciate the work he does?
Contemporary Music – *Worship* CD:
  Song Title: *"Open the Eyes of My Heart"* – Track 5
Traditional Music – *Ryman Gospel Reunion* CD:
  Song Title: *"Out of His Great Love"* – Track 9

Chapter 16: Day 3

A Mother's Love

> A baby is born with a need to be loved –
> and never outgrows it.
> - Frank A. Clark

Rich and our son, Wyatt, were going fishing, and excitement was in the air. Wyatt's face beamed, as he happily skipped back and forth from the house to the suburban to help pack. It seemed like just yesterday that Wyatt was a baby. Now, as I watched Wyatt be his daddy's right hand "man", I knew I was witnessing a turning point in life.

Wyatt wasn't my baby anymore. He had somehow skipped on to the next stage of life, without me even knowing it. As I saw him strain to lift heavy things and hustle to do his daddy's calling, my heart swelled with mixed emotions. I was glad that he was growing up to be a hard worker, but I was a little sad too, because he seemed to need me a little less than he did before.

This thought seemed punctuated by the fact that Wyatt forgot to tell me goodbye. I knew they were in a hurry, but my heart still ached. Suddenly, the suburban made a u-turn back into our driveway. Wyatt hopped out, his little arms pumping as he ran to me.

"I forgot to hug you goodbye, Mom! Love ya!" he said as he planted a big kiss on my cheek. I hugged him tightly, and I felt as if my heart would burst. I guess needing me a little less didn't mean loving me a little less. As I watched him go, I tucked the memory away, as only mothers can do.

BIBLE CONNECTION:
THE LOVE BETWEEN ELISHA AND HIS MOTHER

Elijah put his cloak on Elisha to show him that he would succeed him as prophet. Elisha left his oxen to run after Elijah, but then he stopped, saying, "Let me kiss my father and mother goodbye, and then I will come with you." After doing so, he set out to follow Elijah. (I Kings 19:19-21)

PERSONAL CONNECTION
ROLE #3: MOTHER

Elisha knew that following Elijah was the right thing to do, but he still wanted to say goodbye to his parents. I'm sure Elisha's mother felt happy that her son would be God's prophet, but sad that he was leaving her side. As mothers, we often feel these mixed emotions. We want our children to be strong disciples for God, but we have a hard time letting them go. The years that we can be together with our children go by so quickly. Let's make sure that we make the most of them, so our children know a mother's love is something they'll always carry with them, even when we have to be apart.

 ## A WELCOME RETREAT

Prayer to Share (with children): *Lord, I love the time I spend with my children, and I love being their mother.*
Question: Do your children know how blessed you feel to be their mother and to be loved by them?
Contemporary Music – *Worship* CD:
  Song Title: *"Open the Eyes of My Heart"* – Track 5
Traditional Music – *Ryman Gospel Reunion* CD:
  Song Title: *"Out of His Great Love"* – Track 9

Chapter 16: Day 4

Lasting Love

> Where there is lasting love, there is family.
> - Shere Hite

"Just come and live with us," my sister Carrie said, as I sobbed to her on the phone. A million thoughts raced through my mind. *Change colleges? Leave my friends? Move to a different city? Did I really need that big of a change? Yes, I did.*

I'd made some poor choices in college… in my friends, in my boyfriends, and in my activities. My boyfriend had just broken up with me. I felt desperately alone, and I didn't know what to do.

"Think about it," I heard Carrie say. "You know you're always welcome here. I love you, and I think a change would do you good. It'll be just like when we were growing up. So, why not?" Her words still hung in the air, as I said goodbye.

I thought, *Why **does** she love me?* I hadn't done a good job of calling her, or going home to see her in the past two years. Still, she was always faithful; with letters, phone calls, and visits. I didn't deserve it, and I knew it.

I moved in with my sister and brother-in-law at the end of that school year. Mike and Carrie were a newly married couple. I'm sure having a young roommate was the last thing they wanted, but they welcomed me anyway. The change in me was gradual, but they were patient with me. They repeatedly told me how much they loved me, and the hopelessness I had felt began to fade away. I started going to church again, and I slowly found my way back to God.

Bible Connection:
Lasting Love for the Prodigal Son

Jesus told this parable: A son took his share of his father's inheritance and spent it all on wild living. He was working as a hired man and starving to death when he decided it would be better to go back and work for his father. While the son was still a long way off, his father saw him and ran to him, throwing his arms around him and kissing him. The father gave a celebration to show how much he still loved his son and to show how glad he was that his son who had been lost was found. (Luke 15:11-32)

Personal Connection
Role #4: Teacher

Our children will do and say things that are hurtful or embarrassing to us. During difficult times today, teach your children that although you didn't like their behavior, you do still love them. Show them that you have a lasting love that will stand the test of time.

 A Welcome Retreat

Prayer to Share (with children): *My children are one of the best gifts you've given me. I love them so much!*
Question: Do your children know that you will always love them, no matter what they have done?
Contemporary Music – *Worship* CD:
  Song Title: *"Open the Eyes of My Heart"* – Track 5
Traditional Music – *Ryman Gospel Reunion* CD:
  Song Title: *"Out of His Great Love"* – Track 9

Chapter 16: Day 5

Reflecting on Love

Role #1: Christian Woman
What would help you have a deeper relationship with your Heavenly Father?

Role #2: Wife
Ask your husband when he has felt most loved by you. Have him tell you why.

Role #3: Mother
Take time to think about what you love most about each of your children. Share it with them.

Role #4: Teacher
As you discipline your children today, focus on always ending each encounter with the overall feeling that you love them.

 A Welcome Retreat

Prayer to Share: *Lord, help me to show more love as a Christian woman, a wife, a mother, and a teacher.*

Contemporary Music: *"Open the Eyes of My Heart"*
  Music Connection: When you open your heart and mind, you can see God at work in your life. God loves you more than anything. He wants to pour out His love on you.

Traditional Music: *"Out of His Great Love"*
  Music Connection: No one has a greater love for you than God does. Your salvation is possible only because of His great love. Remember to give Him your love in return. It's the least He deserves for being a loving God.

If you trust in God and yourself,
you can surmount every obstacle.
Do not yield to restless anxiety.
One must not always be asking
what may happen to one in life,
but one must advance,
fearlessly and bravely.

- Otto von Bismarck

Prepare Your Heart

Prayer:
As a Christian woman, a wife, a mother, and a teacher, help me to trust in You with all of my heart.

Role #1: Christian Woman
Trust in the Lord

Role #2: Wife
Trusting Your Marriage Partner

Role #3: Mother
Trusting the Engineer

Role #4: Teacher
Who Can Be Trusted to Teach Our Children?

Contemporary Music Connection:
"Forever"
God's love does not come and go. It endures forever.
He is always faithful, and you can trust Him
to help you carry on through any situation.

Traditional Music Connection:
"I Never Shall Forget the Day"
If you've given your life to Jesus,
put your trust in Him,
and you will feel a peace within.

Chapter 17: Day 1

Trust in the Lord

> All who call on God in true faith,
> earnestly from the heart, will certainly be heard,
> and will receive what they have asked and desired.
> - Martin Luther

I was expecting for the third time, and Rich and I had met at the hospital to hear our baby's heartbeat and see the ultrasound. We were basking in the wonder of it all when the mood changed drastically, as our doctor spotted a fibroid tumor on my uterine artery.

As the doctor began explaining the surgery I'd need to have, the color drained out of Rich's face, and he unsteadily made his way to the door. I saw him disappear into the bathroom down the hall, as the doctor continued to deliver more bad news. He said the fibroid was in a dangerous location, so he wasn't sure if the procedure would work, and without it, I'd probably deliver at 20-24 weeks. Rich was unusually pale as he shakily re-entered the room in time to hear the doctor agreeing to do the surgery that Saturday. We both felt emotionally drained as we left the hospital.

When I got home, I was a total wreck, alternating between being entirely numb and sobbing uncontrollably. I finally pulled myself together and prayed about it. I also called our family members and asked them to pray. After that, a feeling of peace washed over me, and I was able to put my trust in God. The surgery was a success, but I had 6 more hospitalizations, all of which could have resulted in losing our baby. Each time I had a complication, I put my trust in the Lord. By the grace of God, our second son, Riley was born. "Riley" means *valiant, warlike one*, and with God's help, he was able to win the battle for his life.

Bible Connection: Rahab Trusts in the Lord

Rahab put her trust in the Lord when the battle of Jericho was near. She hid two Israelite spies on her roof and saved them from being captured. She believed God ruled the heaven and the earth, and she knew He had already given Jericho to the Israelites. She begged the spies to swear by the Lord that they would spare her and her family's lives. They agreed to this, since Rahab had already shown herself to be trustworthy. Later, when the city of Jericho fell, only Rahab and her family were spared. (Joshua 2:1-14; 6:17)

Personal Connection
Role #1: Christian Woman

Rahab didn't really know God when she put her trust in Him. She could have turned the spies in or revealed their plans, but she chose to trust the Lord instead. As Christian women, we need to ask the Lord for His help as we march into the battles of life. Then, we need to trust that His help is on the way, just as quickly as we finish asking for it.

A Welcome Retreat

Prayer to Share: *Lord, help me to trust in You completely. Help me to pray with the faith that You've already answered my prayer.*
Question: When you ask the Lord for help, do you trust that He will help you?
Contemporary Music – *Worship* CD:
  Song Title: *"Forever"* – Track 1
Traditional Music – *Ryman Gospel Reunion* CD:
  Song Title: *"I Never Shall Forget the Day"* – Track 13

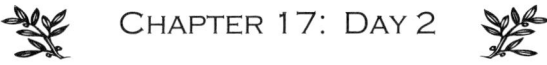

Chapter 17: Day 2

Trusting Your Marriage Partner

> A successful marriage requires falling in love
> many times, always with the same person.
> - Mignon McLaughlin

I first fell in love with Rich because he is a good-looking, honest, hard-working man. Over the years together, I've found more things to love about Rich. For instance, when our car stalled in the middle of a busy, icy intersection, Rich quickly jumped out, pushed the car, and turned the steering wheel to guide us into a nearby parking lot. That day, I fell in love with the way Rich keeps his cool in times of danger.

Then there was the time Rich surprised me by taking me to a concert in a nearby town. I had no idea we were going there, and it was the best concert I've ever been to just because I loved the fact that Rich planned it all on his own.

When Rich and I became parents, I found a lot of new things to love about him. Watching Rich wrestle with our sons, play hide and seek with them, or teach them how to hammer in a nail made me fall in love with him being the father of my children.

One thing I've noticed is that I feel most "in love" with Rich when we are able to spend time together. When we have not spent time together, little seeds of loneliness begin to take root, and we can both get caught up in being too independent. Going on dates and spending time talking alone with one another (even for just 10 minutes) has been time well spent. Taking precious time to do these things has helped keep the trust and love alive in our marriage.

BIBLE CONNECTION:
GOMER WAS NOT TRUSTWORTHY

The prophet Hosea married Gomer, and they had a son together. Gomer had two more children, but it was uncertain who their father was. The names the Lord chose for those children were Lo-Ruhamah, which means *not loved*, and Lo-Ammi, which means *not my people*. (Hosea 1:2-9)

PERSONAL CONNECTION
ROLE #2: WIFE

After Hosea and Gomer's first son was born something went wrong in their marriage. Something caused Gomer to go outside of their marriage commitment. The names God chose for Hosea's children show His contempt for adultery and the dishonesty that goes hand and hand with it. As wives, let's remember that the times in our marriage that we are too busy to be together are usually the times we need to be together the most. Keeping trust and love alive in our marriage requires time together. More years together should bring more ways to love each other. Otherwise, our love will begin to be a memory of the past, and like Gomer and Hosea, we may be left wondering what went wrong.

 A WELCOME RETREAT

Prayer to Share (with husband): *Lord, help my husband and I to keep trust and love alive in our marriage by spending time together.*

Question: How much time do you spend alone with your husband?

Contemporary Music – *Worship* CD:
  Song Title: *"Forever"* – Track 1

Traditional Music – *Ryman Gospel Reunion* CD:
  Song Title: *"I Never Shall Forget the Day"* – Track 13

Chapter 17: Day 3

Trusting the Engineer

> When a train goes through a tunnel and it gets dark,
> you don't throw away the ticket and jump off.
> You sit still and trust the engineer.
> - Corrie ten Boom

Our whole family was out in the middle of a bean field when we heard the tornado siren. We ran to our truck as the wind and rain whipped around us. My dad drove as fast as he could to the nearest farmhouse, but the trees were bent over, blocking the driveway. Since we couldn't drive out of the storm, we pulled over. My dad stayed in the truck to move it and make sure it wouldn't blow over on us. He told my mom to take us three girls and go lay flat in the deepest ditch we could find. My mom trusted my father completely, and she did exactly what he asked her to do.

Mom had us sing *Jesus Loves Me,* as she prayed for our family's safety. The truck moved back and forth in the wind, and trees broke in half as if they were toothpicks. My jacket ripped off of me and whipped high into the sky. Then, just as quickly as it had begun, it was over. It was eerily calm, and the sky was a greenish-gray.

Dad called for us to get back into the truck, and we drove for miles, navigating around washed out bridges and debris covered roads. As we came into our driveway, we saw our barn had been lifted up and set back down a foot off of its foundation. It was a scary sight, and I'll always remember how my mother put her trust in God that day. When the winds began blowing, she knew enough to sit still, take time to pray, sing praises, and let the Engineer take control.

BIBLE CONNECTION:
A WIDOW TRUSTS GOD TO SAVE HER CHILDREN

A widow put her trust in God when she begged His prophet, Elisha, for help. A creditor was coming to take her two sons as slaves, and she didn't know what to do. Elisha asked what she had in her house, and she said she only had a little oil. Elisha told her to ask all of her neighbors for empty jars. When she got home from collecting the jars, she shut the door behind her and her sons. As her sons brought the jars to her, she kept pouring oil into them. When all of the jars were full, the oil stopped flowing. Elisha told her to sell the oil and pay her debts so her and her sons could live on what was left. (II Kings 4:1-7)

PERSONAL CONNECTION
ROLE #3: MOTHER

This widow had been married to a prophet herself, and she knew firsthand how God used prophets to do His work. When her children were in need, she knew to put her trust in the Lord to engineer a plan that would save her family. As mothers, when the circumstances our family faces seem impossible, we should be like this widow and put our trust in the Lord. Then, like my mother, we should be still, pray, sing praises, and wait for the Engineer to do the rest.

 A WELCOME RETREAT

Prayer to Share (with children): *When my children and I face difficult circumstances, help us to put our trust in You.*
Question: Do your children really trust the Lord?
Contemporary Music – *Worship* CD:
 Song Title: *"Forever"* – Track 1
Traditional Music – *Ryman Gospel Reunion* CD:
 Song Title: *"I Never Shall Forget the Day"* – Track 13

Chapter 17: Day 4

Who Can Be Trusted to Teach Our Children?

> Every mother is like Moses. She does not enter the promised land. She prepares a world she will not see.
> - Pope Paul VI

My grandparents were only educated through the eighth grade. My dad was unable to attend college until later in life, and when he was able to go, he appreciated it greatly. My mom was a teacher, and I was raised to believe that education is a gift. With this kind of upbringing, it made sense when my sisters and I also became teachers. I taught quite happily in the public school for 7 years. Then, my son Wyatt was born, and I began to envision him at my school.

I began watching some teachers around me, and I cringed to think of Wyatt in the teacher's class who belittled certain students. Or, in the teacher's class who had lots of parties, lots of treats, lots of movies, and very little learning. Or, in the class where the teacher lectured all day, never letting the students leave their seats. Or, in the class where the teacher shared he was a homosexual, an evolutionist, or an atheist.

It began to seem that education was not much of a gift without God at the center of it. Maybe that's because God entrusted our children to us, expecting us to teach them about Him. "Schools" were not entrusted with this responsibility, parents were. One of the best gifts we can give our children is a "school" day full of God, with a Christian parent they consider their "teacher". God doesn't just *want* us to train our children to know and love Him – He *expects* it (Proverbs 22:6). This can't happen if most of their days are spent without Him and without us.

BIBLE CONNECTION: BE CAREFUL OF BLIND GUIDES

Jesus told this parable: Can a blind man lead a blind man? Will they not both fall into a pit? A student is not above his teacher, but a student who is fully trained by his teacher, will become like his teacher. So make sure you follow the right teachers and leaders because you will go no further than they do. Look for leaders who will show you more about faith and in whose guidance you can trust. (Luke 6:39-40)

PERSONAL CONNECTION
ROLE #4: TEACHER

Anyone who teaches our children has the power to lead them either closer to God, or further away from Him. We need to make sure we are not entrusting "blind guides" with the all-important task of teaching our children. When we choose to teach our own children about God, we accept our God-given responsibility to do so (Deuteronomy 6:6-9). As teachers of our children, we'll never give a more important lesson than the lesson that God is most important. If that is the only lesson our children learn from "schooling", it will have been a total success.

 A WELCOME RETREAT

Prayer to Share (with children): *Lord, You've entrusted me to teach my children about You. Help me to do so when we're home, when we're on the road, when we lie down, and when we get up.*
Question: How much time do you personally spend teaching your children about God?
Contemporary Music – *Worship* CD:
  Song Title: *"Forever"* – Track 1
Traditional Music – *Ryman Gospel Reunion* CD:
  Song Title: *"I Never Shall Forget the Day"* – Track 13

Chapter 17: Day 5

Reflecting on Trust

Role #1: Christian Woman
Begin praying with a faith that shows you trust in the Lord. After you pray, trust that His help is on the way, just as quickly as you say "Amen".

Role #2: Wife
When is the last time you went out on a date with your husband? If it's been more than two weeks, make plans for a date this week. (Even coffee and dessert can be a date!)

Role #3: Mother
As a mother, what current situation requires your trust in God? What current situation requires your children to trust in God? Share your situations with each other as much as is appropriate, and commit to praying for one another.

Role #4: Teacher
Have you trusted "blind guides" to teach your children? Choose "guides" and curriculum with Him in mind first.

A Welcome Retreat

Prayer to Share: *As a Christian woman, a wife, a mother, and a teacher, help me to trust in You with all of my heart.*

Contemporary Music: *"Forever"*
  Music Connection: God's love does not come and go. It endures forever. He is always faithful, and you can trust Him to help you carry on through any situation.

Traditional Music: *"I Never Shall Forget the Day"*
  Music Connection: If you've given your life to Jesus, put your trust in Him, and you will feel a peace within.

Laughter is the jam
on the toast of life.
It adds flavor,
keeps it from being too dry,
and makes it easier to swallow.

- Diane Johnson

Prepare Your Heart

Prayer:
*Lord, help me find the joy You bring to me
as a Christian woman, wife, mother, and teacher.*

Role #1: Christian Woman
Unexpected Joy and Humor

Role #2: Wife
Finding Joy in Marriage

Role #3: Mother
The Right and Wrong Time to Laugh

Role #4: Teacher
Finding Joy in Teaching about God

Contemporary Music Connection:
"Forever"
When you feel joy, it is a gift from God.
Simply the fact that He loves you, forever,
is reason enough to sing praises to Him.

Traditional Music Connection:
"I'm Feeling Fine"
When Jesus is your companion all of the time,
the joy you feel in your soul comes from Him.

Chapter 18: Day 1
Unexpected Joy and Humor

> Joy is what happens to us when we allow ourselves to
> recognize how good things really are.
> - Marianne Williamson

My sister Carrie and I were on our way to the airport. It was a 3-hour drive, and we were short on time, which is probably why we went through a yellow stoplight. Unfortunately, the lady on our left didn't see us, and she ran into our car. A policeman came, insurance information was exchanged, and we were told to find a local car repair shop. However, Carrie and I were two sisters bound for a plane to visit our other sister; the damages didn't look *that* bad. Our car had a big "V"-shaped gash on the driver's door, and part of the trim and a piece of the fender were both sticking out. Carrie and I looked at each other like Bonnie and Clyde, and she said, "Are you thinking what I'm thinking?"

"You know I am!" I replied. She ripped off the trim, I yanked off the fender piece, and we were on our way. Cold winter air began gushing in the door. We layered on more and more clothes from our luggage, and I began scraping the ice off the inside of the windshield.

When we made it to our gate at the airport, the lady told us we could run down the hall and knock on the door of the plane. We thought she was kidding. She wasn't. As we ran down the hall and knocked on the plane's door, it slowly opened, and the passengers stared at us in awe. We must have been quite a sight with our red faces and many layers of mismatched clothes. Whenever we think back to how God helped us get on that plane, we can't help but smile.

Bible Connection:
Rhoda's Unexpectedly Joyful to See Peter

A servant girl named Rhoda went to answer the knock at the door. When she recognized she was hearing Peter's voice, she was so overjoyed she ran back without opening the door. She told the people who were there praying for Peter that he was at the door. They thought she was out of her mind because King Herod had put Peter in prison. However, when the people heard more knocking, they opened the door and were astonished to see Peter. When Peter told them how the Lord had brought him out of prison, everyone was filled with joy. (Acts 12:4, 12-17)

Personal Connection
Role #1: Christian Woman

Joy and humor can come at the least expected moments. Rhoda and a room full of saddened Christians found joy when Peter unexpectedly knocked on their door. Carrie and I found humor after a car accident when we unexpectedly knocked on a plane's door. As Christian women, let's seek out joy and humor in life. When we find it, let's praise God for providing those unexpected moments that remind us of how good things really are.

 A Welcome Retreat

Prayer to Share: *Lord, help me not to be too busy to miss those unexpected moments of joy and humor that You provide in my life.*
Question: Are you too busy to take time for joy and humor in your life?
Contemporary Music – *Worship* CD:
  Song Title: *"Forever"* – Track 1
Traditional Music – *Ryman Gospel Reunion* CD:
  Song Title: *"I'm Feeling Fine"* – Track 16

Chapter 18: Day 2

Finding Joy in Marriage

> Grief can take care of itself, but to get the full value of joy, we must have somebody to divide it with.
> - Mark Twain

Rich's sense of humor is one of the things I love most about him – most of the time. When I first got my teaching job, I asked Rich to help me correct a few students' papers and hang a few things around the classroom.

The next day at school, a student told me he liked all of the smiley faces drawn in *every* letter "o" on his paper. I held back a laugh as I imagined Rich decorating every "o" on that paper. Then, another student brought me her paper to show me the misspelled comment "Nise Job" at the top. I didn't feel like laughing about that one. A third student brought me his paper to show me the misspelled comment "Turifec". Still another distraught student brought me his paper. He'd missed every answer, and the comment at the top was, "Don't you know this stuff? Study more!" That was a terrible comment, but at least it was spelled right.

As I began seizing students' corrected papers, a blurred vision of the bulletin board came into view. It said "Grate Pappers". That's when I noticed many bewildered students sitting in "time out" around the room. Apparently, *someone* had moved their stoplights to red, which meant they needed to go to time out. I never had Rich help me with my work at school again. Now, I am able to look back at that day and laugh. After ten years of marriage, Rich still surprises me. I hope to look ahead to many more years of fun with Rich, and I'm thankful for each day we laugh together.

BIBLE CONNECTION:
SOLOMON AND HIS WIFE FOUND JOY TOGETHER

Solomon had many wives, but one wife and he took great joy in their love for one another. Song of Songs is a testimony of this joy, albeit the few times arguments arose. This joy is especially evident when the wife of Solomon said... *Place me like a seal over your heart, like a seal on your arm; for love is as strong as death, its jealousy is unyielding as the grave. It burns like blazing fire, like a mighty flame. Many waters cannot quench love; rivers cannot wash it away.* (Song of Songs 8:6-7a)

PERSONAL CONNECTION
ROLE #2: WIFE

Love keeps the joy of marriage alive. Solomon and his wife understood this, and they worked hard to find joy in the time they spent together. When Rich and I have spent more time laughing than arguing, we find joy that keeps our love alive too. As wives, we need to take time to laugh with our husbands. If all we ever talk about are problems or things of a serious nature, our marriage will be serious and focused on problems. We all want to find joy in life, so let's make sure we find it at home with the one we love.

 A WELCOME RETREAT

Prayer to Share (with husband): *Lord, help my husband and I enjoy marriage by finding laughter and joy in life together.*
Question: When is the last time you and your husband laughed out loud together?
Contemporary Music – *Worship* CD:
  Song Title: *"Forever"* – Track 1
Traditional Music – *Ryman Gospel Reunion* CD:
  Song Title: *"I'm Feeling Fine"* – Track 16

CHAPTER 18: DAY 3

THE RIGHT AND WRONG TIME TO LAUGH

> One loses many laughs by not laughing at oneself.
> - Sara Jeannette Duncan

My dad has a great sense of humor, and he taught me to love to laugh. I've found the best person to laugh at is always myself, since there are endless opportunities to do so. I laughed when my shoulder pad fell out during my first job interview. I also laughed when I flew off the back of a treadmill and "tackled" a football player. I laughed again when I noticed a group of construction workers watching me chase my puppy around the yard, trying to kennel him (in my dress and heels, it took me 30 minutes to catch him).

Laughter has not only helped me through the clumsy, embarrassing times in life; it's also helped me through some difficult times. One of those times was after a surgery I had to remove my uterine fibroid. I think I was so tired of worrying so much and being so emotional, that my sense of humor unfortunately kicked in.

My doctor, who is quite serious in nature, came to ask how I was doing. Since I'd had a glorified c-section, I said, *It wasn't as much fun to deliver a fibroid.* She paused a moment, but then gave no reply. Moving on in her report, she told me she'd found two fibroids instead of one. I said, *So, I had twin fibroids?* No comment. No smile. Then, she said she'd removed them both. I said, *Do you think I may have lost that extra 15 pounds I've been carrying around now?* She looked me straight in the eyes and said very seriously, *Julie, fibroids don't weigh that much.* After that, I quit joking around and thanked her for doing my surgery. I'd figured out that I might have been laughing at the wrong time, with the wrong person.

BIBLE CONNECTION: SARAH LAUGHS AT THE WRONG TIME

Sarah laughed when she overheard the Lord tell her husband, Abraham, that she'd have a son within a year. She was old and past the age of childbearing, and she thought it was too late for her to have the pleasure of having a son. The Lord asked Abraham why Sarah had laughed, saying, "Is anything too hard for the Lord?" Sarah was afraid that she'd been heard laughing, so she lied and said she didn't laugh, but the Lord said, "Yes, you did." (Genesis 18:10-15)

PERSONAL CONNECTION
ROLE #3: MOTHER

Sarah got caught laughing at the wrong time, with the wrong Person. She lied to try to cover it up, but of course, that was impossible. Perhaps as a reminder, Sarah's son was named "Isaac", which means "he laughs". As mothers, let's take time to laugh with our children. Let's also take time to discuss the right and wrong times to laugh. I'm living proof it may take us just as long as them to learn the difference.

 A WELCOME RETREAT

Prayer to Share (with children): *Lord, help our home to be filled with laughter, and help us to be laughing at the right things.*
Question: Is your home a place of love and laughter?
Contemporary Music – *Worship* CD:
  Song Title: *"Forever"* – Track 1
Traditional Music – *Ryman Gospel Reunion* CD:
  Song Title: *"I'm Feeling Fine"* – Track 16

Chapter 18: Day 4

Finding Joy in Teaching about God

> One laugh of a child will make
> the holiest day more sacred still.
> - Robert G. Ingersoll

Wyatt and I had just finished reading the Bible story about John the Baptist baptizing Jesus. Wyatt takes things very literally, so I asked him to retell the story. Wyatt began by saying, "Jesus came to the river to be baptized by John, so John baptized Jesus." *Right!* I thought. Then, Wyatt said laughingly in a confused voice, "A dove came down next, and dropped God's Spirit on Jesus' head. That had to hurt, but you seemed to think it was a good thing, Mom." As I explained the real meaning of *God's Spirit came down in the form of a dove and landed upon Jesus,* we laughed together.

Another time, Wyatt and I were reading about Peter Rabbit. The book was about Reddy Fox constantly trying to catch Peter Rabbit. After Wyatt attended Sunday school, I asked him to tell me what he'd learned there. Wyatt said he'd learned about Jesus walking on the water, Peter walking on the water, Peter starting to sink, and Jesus saving him. I said, "Wasn't that a neat story about Peter trusting God?"

Wyatt said, "Yeah, but all I could think is *I'm so glad Reddy Fox wasn't in the boat.*" Wyatt had combined the story about Peter Rabbit with the story about Peter the disciple. I laughed at the thought of Wyatt imagining Peter Rabbit walking on the water. I told Wyatt that the story was not about Peter Rabbit, and he had a good laugh too. Teaching Wyatt about the Bible has brought us laughter as his confusions are cleared, and joy, as he understands more.

Wyatt may not always grow in Bible knowledge as quickly as I wish at times, but spiritual growth is not something to be forced. It is something to be lovingly nurtured, over time.

Bible Connection:
The Joy of Nurturing a Growing Seed

A plant's growth can't be rushed, and neither can spiritual growth. Jesus told this parable to illustrate this: A man scatters seed on the ground. Night and day, whether he sleeps or gets up, the seed sprouts and grows, though he does not know how. All by itself the soil produces grain – first the stalk, then the head, then the full kernel in the head. As soon as the grain is ripe, he puts the sickle to it, because the harvest has come. (Mark 4:26-29)

Personal Connection
Role #4: Teacher

As teachers of our children, we can take joy in helping our children grow, by teaching them about the Bible and by helping them through their confusions. We must tell them the Word of God, but we must also depend on the power of God to produce the fruit. Then, when the time is right, we can all enjoy the Lord's harvest together.

 A Welcome Retreat

Prayer to Share (with children): *Lord, help me to teach my children about You, so we can be together forever.*
Question: Do you take time to celebrate the joys of your children's spiritual growth?
Contemporary Music – *Worship* CD:
  Song Title: *"Forever"* – Track 1
Traditional Music – *Ryman Gospel Reunion* CD:
  Song Title: *"I'm Feeling Fine"* – Track 16

Chapter 18: Day 5

Reflecting on Joy and Humor

Role #1: Christian Woman
What brings you joy and humor in your life? Praise God for providing unexpected happiness at just the right times.

Role #2: Wife
Do you and your husband laugh together? Make laughter a part of your marriage by sharing the joys of life as often as you share the problems of life.

Role #3: Mother
How often can your children be heard laughing in your home? If it's often, and *everyone* is laughing, good for you! If it's not very often, know they will find it somewhere outside the home, and it may be the wrong kind of laughter.

Role #4: Teacher
Do your children know the joy your personal relationship with God brings you? Make sure your children see your spiritual growth, so they can take joy in growing as well.

 A Welcome Retreat

Prayer to Share: *Lord, help me find the joy You bring to me as a Christian woman, wife, mother, and teacher.*
Contemporary Music: *"Forever"*
  Music Connection: When you feel joy, it is a gift from God. Simply the fact that He loves you, forever, is reason enough to sing praises to Him.
Traditional Music: *"I'm Feeling Fine"*
  Music Connection: When Jesus is your companion all of the time, the joy you feel in your soul comes from Him.

DEAR READER,

Now it's time to say goodbye. Perhaps we'll meet again, maybe in another book if the Lord calls me to write one. Either way, I enjoyed our time together. Sometimes life gets somewhat lonely when you're doing things a little differently from others around you. I prayed for you as I wrote this book, and you became real to me as I imagined who you might be, how you might be feeling, and what you might be doing.

I feel a kinship with you because I already know the most important thing about you – you are the kind of person who loves our Lord and takes time out of your busy life to be with Him. If I knew nothing else about you, that would still be enough to make us friends. I pray the Lord will lift you and your family up as you choose to live your life for Him.

It is my greatest prayer that this book brings glory to God. If this book helped you to have special time with our Lord and Savior, then my prayers have been answered because you have brought glory to God by spending time with Him. If you have been blessed by doing this devotional, and you would like to write me a note, I would love to hear from you. You can reach me at the following addresses:

    Julie Grosz
    47473 248th St.
    Dell Rapids, SD 57022
    e-mail address: rjgrosz@siouxvalley.net

Books authored by me or my family may also be purchased at www.heartofdakota.com.

Blessings to you!
Julie Grosz

Scripture References

> **KEY:** **Role #1** = Christian Woman (links with women from the Bible)
> **Role #2** = Wife (links with couples from the Bible)
> **Role #3** = Mother (links with mothers from the Bible)
> **Role #4** = Teacher of Your Children (links with Jesus' Parables)

Chapter One: Attitude
   Role #1: A Poor Widow Has a Reverent Attitude
        Mark 12:42-44
   Role #2: Acsah and Her Husband Work Together
        Judges 1:12-15
   Role #3: A Mother's Persistence Saves Her Son
        II Kings 4:8-37
   Role #4: A Humble Servant Has a Good Attitude
        Luke 17:7-10

Chapter Two: Meaningful Relationships
   Role #1: Mary Knows What's Needed Most
        Luke 10:38-42
   Role #2: Adam and Eve Fill Each Other's Needs
        Genesis 2:18-24
   Role #3: Lois and Eunice's Legacy of Faith
        II Timothy 1:15; II Timothy 4:14-15
   Role #4: Jesus, Our Shepherd, Gives Us Security
        John 10:14-16

Chapter Three: Attraction
   Role #1: Bernice and Agrippa Make an Appearance
        Acts 25:13-27; 26:25-31
   Role #2: Herodias' and Herod's Roving Attraction
        Mark 6:17-29
   Role #3: Dinah's Attraction to Trouble
        Genesis 34:1-25
   Role #4: A Pharisee Worries about Appearances
        Luke 18:9-14

Chapter Four: Stress and Pressure
  Role #1: Lydia Spends Time on Important "Business"
    Acts 16:14-15, 40
  Role #2: A Wife of Noble Character
    Proverbs 31:10-12, 27-28
  Role #3: Jochebed Says "Yes" to More Family Time
    Exodus 2:1-10; Numbers 26:59
  Role #4: Invited Guests Are Too Busy to Come
    Luke 14:16-24

Chapter Five: Strength of Character
  Role #1: Anna "Tells It Like It Is"
    Luke 2:22, 36-38
  Role #2: Two Queens Have Different Approaches
    Esther 1- 7
  Role #3: Two Women Show Strength of Faith
    Matt. 27:56, 61; 28:1; Mark 15:40, 47; 16:1;
    Luke 24:10; John 19:25
  Role #4: A Strong Or a Weak Foundation
    Matthew 7:24-27

Chapter Six: Shortcomings
  Role #1: Bathsheba's Bath Results in Sin
    II Samuel 11:2-27; 12:14-19
  Role #2: The Shortage of Wine at a Wedding
    John 2:1-10
  Role #3: A Mother Makes a Selfish Request
    Matthew 20:20-27
  Role #4: Being Prepared Going into Battle
    Luke 14:31-33

Chapter Seven: Differences
  Role #1: A Woman Shows David's Not So Different
    2 Samuel 14:1-21
  Role #2: Zechariah and Elizabeth Think Differently
    Luke 1:6-25
  Role #3: Isaac and Rebekah Favor Different Sons
    Genesis 25:27-28; 27:1-10
  Role #4: Being Different by Being Jesus' Disciples
    John 15:5-8

Chapter Eight: Jealousy, Envy, and Greed
Role #1: Jezebel's Jealousy, Envy, and Greed
I Kings 21:1-23
Role #2: Jealousy Between Rachel and Leah
Genesis 29:30-31; 30:1-2
Role #3: Bathsheba's Son Follows His Dad's Lead
I Kings 1:17, 29-30; 2:1-3; 3:3
Role #4: A Rich Man Learns the Cost of Greed
Luke 16:19-26

Chapter Nine: Worry
Role #1: A Widow of Zarapheth Pushes Worry Aside
I Kings 17:9-15
Role #2: Michal and David Worry about Relatives
I Samuel 18:20-29
Role #3: Hannah Could Have Let Worry Take Root
I Samuel 1:11, 19, 24; 2:19, 26
Role #4: Sowing the Seed of the Word of God
Luke 8:4-8

Chapter Ten: Sadness
Role #1: A Sinful Woman Who Wept at Jesus' Feet
Luke 7:36-39; 47-50
Role #2: The Sadness of the Parents of a Blind Son
John 9:1-7
Role #3: Rizpah Mourns the Loss of Her Sons
II Samuel 21:8-14
Role #4: The Good Samaritan Cares for a Stranger
Luke 10:30-37

Chapter Eleven: Confusion
Role #1: A Young Maid Solves Naaman's Problem
II Kings 5:2-5, 9-14
Role #2: Confusion During Abram and Sarai's Trip
Genesis 12:10-20
Role #3: Belshazzar's Mother Seeks Daniel's Help
Daniel 5:1-30
Role #4: A Friend Persists to Do the Right Thing
Luke 11:5-8

Chapter Twelve: Thoughts
  Role #1: A Woman Discovers Jesus Is Thoughtful
        John 4:7-19, 28-29
  Role #2: Michal's Thoughts Become Words
        II Samuel 6:14-23
  Role #3: Mary's Thoughts about Being a Mother
        Luke 1:30-32, 46-49
  Role #4: A Rich Man's Selfish Thoughts
        Luke 12:16-21

Chapter Thirteen: Achievement
  Role #1: Miriam Wants More Credit Than Moses
        Numbers 12:1-15
  Role #2: Noah's Wife Gets on the Boat
        Genesis 6:18; 7:11-13; 8:13-16
  Role #3: How King Sisera's Mother Rated Success
        Judges 4:2-3, 21; 5:28-30
  Role #4: Guests Covet Honored Wedding Seats
        Luke 14:7-10

Chapter Fourteen: Organization
  Role #1: Wise Hearted Women Get Organized
        Exodus 35:25-26
  Role #2: Abigail Is Deliberate in Her Actions
        I Samuel 25:3-19, 32-33
  Role #3: Jehosheba Plans to Save Joash's Life
        II Kings 11:1-16
  Role #4: A Tower Builder Gets Organized
        Luke 14:28-30

Chapter Fifteen: Anger
  Role #1: A Sick Woman Finds Peace in Jesus
        Mark 5:25-34
  Role #2: Joseph and Mary Are Mistakenly Angry
        Luke 2:41-49
  Role #3: Samson's Waywardness Upsets His Mother
        Judges 13:7-10; 14:1-3
  Role #4: Just When You Think You've Kicked a Habit
        Matthew 12:43-45

Chapter Sixteen: Love
  Role #1: Mary of Bethany Shows Her Love
      John 12:3-8
  Role #2: Jacob Works to Prove His Love
      Genesis 29:18-30
  Role #3: The Love Between Elisha and His Mother
      I Kings 19:19-21
  Role #4: Lasting Love for the Prodigal Son
      Luke 15:11-32

Chapter Seventeen: Trust
  Role #1: Rahab Trusts in the Lord
      Joshua 2:1-14; 6:17
  Role #2: Gomer Was Not Trustworthy
      Hosea 1:2-9
  Role #3: A Widow Trusts God to Save Her Children
      II Kings 4:1-7
  Role #4: Be Careful of Blind Guides
      Luke 6:39-40

Chapter Eighteen: Time for Joy
  Role #1: Rhoda's Unexpectedly Joyful to See Peter
      Acts 12:4, 12-17
  Role #2: Solomon and His Wife Found Joy Together
      Song of Songs 8:6-7a
  Role #3: Sarah Laughs at the Wrong Time
      Genesis 18:10-15
  Role #4: The Joy of Nurturing a Growing Seed
      Mark 4:26-29

GRANDPA PETE AND GRANDMA JO MELLEMA
MY DAD'S PARENTS

GRANDPA NICK AND GRANDMA EVELYN STAR
MY MOTHER'S PARENTS

KEN AND MARLENE MELLEMA
MY PARENTS

DAVE AND CINDY MADDEN
MY SISTER AND BROTHER-IN-LAW

MIKE AND CARRIE AUSTIN
MY SISTER AND BROTHER-IN-LAW

RICH AND JULIE GROSZ
MY HUSBAND AND I

WYATT AND RILEY GROSZ
MY SONS

MY PARENTS AND ALL THE GRANDCHILDREN (SO FAR)
MOM, ABBIE, DAD, JOSH, ANNA, SHAW, RILEY, COLE, ELIZABETH, GREY, WYATT, RACHEL, AND AARON

Resources:

Smith, Michael W. *Worship*. Provident Music Distribution, Inc. Franklin, TN: Reunion Records, Inc.

Gaither, Bill and Gloria. *Ryman Gospel Reunion*. Alexandria, IN. Gaither Music Co., Inc.